CREATING
GLASS BEADS

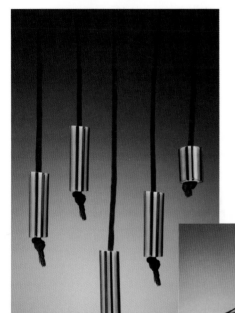

A NEW WORKSHOP TO
EXPAND YOUR BEGINNER SKILLS
AND DEVELOP YOUR ARTISTIC VOICE

Jeri L. Warhaftig

LARK
CRAFTS

An Imprint of Sterling Publishing Co., Inc.
New York

WWW.LARKCRAFTS.COM

editor
Nathalie Mornu

developing editor
Valerie Van Arsdale Shrader

art director
Kathleen Holmes

art assistant
Carol Morse

copy editor
Carol Taylor

photographer
Steve Mann

cover designer
John Barnett

THIS BOOK IS DEDICATED TO MY HUSBAND AND FELLOW BEADMAKER NEIL FABRICANT. OUR SYNERGY HAS AFFORDED ME WONDERFUL ADVENTURES I NEVER ANTICIPATED.

Library of Congress Cataloging-in-Publication Data

Warhaftig, Jeri L.
  Creating glass beads : a new workshop to expand your beginner skills and develop your artistic voice / Jeri L. Warhaftig.—1st ed.
    p. cm.\
  Includes index.
  ISBN 978-1-60059-582-0 (hc-plc : alk. paper)
  1. Glass beads. 2. Glass craft. 3. Glass blowing and working. I. Title.
  TT298.W36985 2011
  748.8'5—dc22

2010030979

10 9 8 7 6 5 4 3 2 1

First Edition

Published by Lark Crafts, An Imprint of Sterling Publishing Co., Inc.
387 Park Avenue South, New York, NY 10016

Text © 2011, Jeri L. Warhaftig
Photography © 2011, Lark Crafts, An Imprint of Sterling Publishing Co., Inc. unless otherwise specified
Illustrations © 2011, Lark Crafts, An Imprint of Sterling Publishing Co., Inc. unless otherwise specified

Distributed in Canada by Sterling Publishing, c/o Canadian Manda Group, 165 Dufferin Street
Toronto, Ontario, Canada M6K 3H6

Distributed in the United Kingdom by GMC Distribution Services,
Castle Place, 166 High Street, Lewes, East Sussex, England BN7 1XU

Distributed in Australia by Capricorn Link (Australia) Pty Ltd.,
P.O. Box 704, Windsor, NSW 2756 Australia

The written instructions, photographs, designs, patterns, and projects in this volume are intended for the personal use of the reader and may be reproduced for that purpose only. Any other use, especially commercial use, is forbidden under law without written permission of the copyright holder.

Every effort has been made to ensure that all the information in this book is accurate. However, due to differing conditions, tools, and individual skills, the publisher cannot be responsible for any injuries, losses, and other damages that may result from the use of the information in this book.

If you have questions or comments about this book, please contact:
Lark Crafts, 67 Broadway, Asheville, NC 28801
828-253-0467

Manufactured in China

ISBN 13: 978-1-60059-582-0

For information about custom editions, special sales, premium, and corporate purchases, please contact the Sterling Special Sales Department at 800-805-5489 or specialsales@sterlingpub.com.

For information about desk and examination copies available to college and university professors, submit requests to academic@larkbooks.com. Our complete policy can be found at www.larkcrafts.com.

Contents

Welcome to My Studio, Once Again

Welcome to my workshop in intermediate glass beadmaking. You most likely find yourself entranced by the magical properties of glass, its vibrant color palette, and its maddening but exciting ability to morph from liquid to solid. Perhaps you found your way here via my earlier book, *Glass Bead Workshop*. Maybe you picked up this book because you love glass beads, beadmaking, or art glass. Whether you're a student, a collector, or a beadmaker, this is the book for you.

The art of glass beadmaking continues to grow and evolve worldwide. Commercially, glass beads of greatly improving quality are now being manufactured in the Czech Republic, China, India, Italy, and elsewhere. In the studio art world, working artists have established flourishing studios in the United States, and in other visually and artistically rich locations such as Japan, Mexico, Turkey, New Zealand, South Africa, and the United Kingdom. More studios and more teachers have resulted in more excited and energized students, seeking in large part to move past beginner skills to establish their own body of work, their own artistic identity, and a style that they can consider personal to themselves.

Creating Glass Beads is my modest contribution to that effort. Ten beadmaking projects introduce techniques, tools, and materials that will be new to some students. The technical appendices introduce the use of resin and mirroring in conjunction with glass beads, for example. But traditional materials are used in novel ways, too, for different and intriguing artistic results. These projects aren't ends in themselves, but steps along the way in the personal artistic journey of each bead artist.

Who Am I?

For more than 15 years, I've been a student and teacher of glass beadmaking, a collector of glass beads, and a participant in the not-for-profit and online glass beadmaking communities. I believe in an open and productive exchange of knowledge and ideas, and chime in on forum dialogues about glass beads and beadmaking materials on both www.isgb.org (the website of the International Society of Glass Beadmakers, an organization dedicated to educating about and promoting glass beadmaking) and www.lampworketc.com. Over the years, I interfaced with hundreds of fellow bead instructors during my tenure on the Education Committee of the ISGB. In 2008 I published my first book, a collection of 10 workshop sessions, each focused on a single bead project.

Since then, I've continued to travel and teach, using that first book as the basis for my classes in intermediate beadmaking. This book is the culmination of my experiences in recent years. Since that first book was published, two things

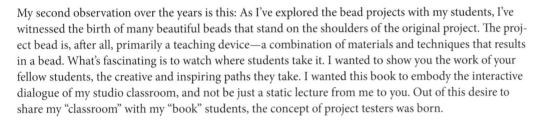

have struck me particularly. First, time and again, students have expressed their fascination with the last chapter of *Glass Bead Workshop*, Near Misses, a collection of beads that didn't quite measure up. Some were technically flawed, others just ugly. As I had hoped, showcasing my own mistakes helped my students to see that their unsatisfactory beads weren't failures, but essential steps in the creative process. Beads that don't work can teach us a great deal. So, once again, I've saved all my prototype project beads to show in this book. Looking back, they range from hideous to embarrassing to downright unique. I intend to share them all. Perhaps you can avoid my mistakes, while making some of your own.

My second observation over the years is this: As I've explored the bead projects with my students, I've witnessed the birth of many beautiful beads that stand on the shoulders of the original project. The project bead is, after all, primarily a teaching device—a combination of materials and techniques that results in a bead. What's fascinating is to watch where students take it. I wanted to show you the work of your fellow students, the creative and inspiring paths they take. I wanted this book to embody the interactive dialogue of my studio classroom, and not be just a static lecture from me to you. Out of this desire to share my "classroom" with my "book" students, the concept of project testers was born.

The Project Testers

For this new book, I set out to recruit a group of intermediate beadmakers to serve as my Project Testers. I needed people who could make symmetrical beads, who worked on dual-fuel torches, and who had ready access to tools and equipment. Just as important, they needed to be adventuresome and willing to move outside their comfort zone to try new things.

Their role was to try out the project beads—to follow my instructions and see what they came up with. Fourteen talented volunteers from all over the globe showed up for work. (You can read a little about them in Appendix D, The Project Testers, on page 141.) They each received a draft of each chapter as it was submitted to the publisher, including a photo of the finished bead and a set of written instructions. (They didn't get the step-by-step photos, which were taken much later in the book-production process.) They also got a little packet of goodies from my studio, things they might need for the projects: some cool murrini, a nugget of aventurine frit, an intense black stringer, a little glow glass frit, a Puffy Mandrel.

Working without how-to photos, the Project Testers found their own way through my tutorials, producing wonderful beads and creative new directions. Some faithfully repeated my designs. Others incorporated part of a project bead into styles of their own. Still others ignored my instructions completely and made their own use of the project materials. Their participation improved every project in the book. They pushed me to innovate and to address issues I hadn't discerned. At the end of every chapter, you'll see the beads they made and read about the challenges they faced. I think you'll find those pages to be some of the most useful and inspiring in the book. I'm deeply grateful for their generosity.

Whether or not you're familiar with the tools, techniques, and materials in this book, you will find exciting and new information that will enable you to improve your beadmaking skills and help you find your artistic voice. You need little more than basic tools and ingenuity to get started. If you lack a project's "ingredients" think about a novel substitute, or design the bead to circumvent that element. You can also turn to the Project Testers for inspiration. In their beads you'll encounter many variations on my themes.

The Basics

Creating Glass Beads is designed for artists who have already mastered beginning beadmaking skills. Still, before we move on to apply those skills in more challenging and innovative ways, it's helpful to have a mutual jumping-off point. After reviewing some familiar tools and materials, I'll give you an overview of how a basic studio is equipped, followed by a reminder about safety—a little nudge that always bears repeating! Finally, I'll suggest how to use this book.

Tools and Materials

At the beginning of each chapter—or tutorial session—you'll find a list of the specialized tools and materials that you'll want to have available if you intend to duplicate the project bead exactly. In the text of the chapters, I suggest possible substitutes, or ways to work around the lack of a particular item. Each chapter assumes, however, that your studio space is equipped with "the basics."

Although I haven't seen any formal research on the subject, I'm fairly certain that there's a high correlation between beadmakers and tool junkies. Most of us seem to amass large numbers of tools, many of which are duplicative in their functions. For me, this is part of the never-ending search for a better tool—one that will perform just like the one I have but perhaps will be more durable, more comfortable in my hand, or just more elegant to look at and use. Whatever the reason, I have a *lot* of tools.

A variety of mandrels coated in bead release

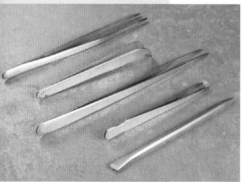

An assortment of handmade tweezers and a steel pick, all made by artist Amnon Elbaz

In part I blame my tool fascination on my friends Amnon Elbaz and Craig Milliron, beadmakers who are tool innovators. Craig is always tempting me with new tools such as specialized marvers or new sifters. Amnon has created several handmade tools for me that I won't let out of my sight. He also created the first Puffy Mandrel (see page 63) and the Baz Box that I use for metal leaf and foil (see pages 15 and 16). Similarly, my husband, Neil Fabricant, is fond of innovative tools and happily brings home whatever device has

been newly developed for use with glass. All of this enables me to experiment with the newest materials, ultimately focusing on what is most suited to my glasswork.

Although I love all of these tools, the fact is, all you need to make great beads are some basic hand tools. The others are largely optional and are employed as much for the pleasure in the using as for the results they achieve. If you don't own a particular tool, find a creative substitute or borrow one from a friend, and don't let that slow you down.

BASIC HAND TOOLS

Mandrels Most of the project beads are made on mandrels that are ³⁄₃₂ inch (2 mm) in diameter. These are steel welding rods marked 308L, which I purchase in bulk. They come in 3-foot (91.4 cm) lengths, which I cut into 12-inch (30.5 cm) pieces with a bolt cutter. I also cut a few shorter lengths to use in projects like the Glass Memento bead (page 94), which requires a second, shorter mandrel. (You can also buy the mandrels precut.) The cut ends need to be briefly ground, so that there's no bur on the end to interfere with removing the bead. The ³⁄₃₂-inch (2 mm) mandrel is comfortable for me, but the projects could be made on other sizes, as well.

Bead release I use a flame-dry bead release. If I want to, I can dip a mandrel in it, dry it immediately in the flame, and make a bead on the spot. (Typically, I let my mandrels dry overnight rather than flame-drying them, but it's nice to have that option.) Flame-drying seems to be least successful on hollow mandrels or mandrels larger than ³⁄₃₂ inch (2 mm) in diameter; dry these overnight if you can. For the big-hole mandrels used in the Glass Memento bead, try a bead release with superior holding power, whether or not it's flame-dryable. Even though the bead may be tough to remove, it will be less likely to break free of the release while you're working in the flame.

Tweezers You'll routinely need a pair of serrated and a pair of nonserrated tweezers. My nonserrated tweezers have pointed tips. Tweezers need not be expensive. They'll last a very long time if you're careful to keep them out of the flame and routinely quench them in water after they touch hot glass. If you expose tweezers to the direct heat of the flame, they're likely to melt or deform and will definitely stick to your glass. The exception is when you're picking up small murrini (see page 43) or other bits of glass for adding to a bead. To avoid shocking the glass, briefly waft the tweezers through the cooler part of the flame to warm them. This might discolor the metal, but it won't do any real harm.

Knife A small kitchen or paring knife is my favorite tool on my bench. I have one style that's comfortable in my hand, and I buy sets of five very inexpensively. That way, when a student admires mine, I can give her one of her own and keep my favorite for me. Again, this is a tool that I use near, but never in, the flame, and if it touches hot glass, I always quench it immediately.

Marvers My torch is equipped with a torch-mounted marver. Although this isn't essential, I use the marver's lip to prewarm small components such as murrini, and sometimes steady my wrist on the edge of the marver when doing detail work. My marver is connected to the torch with an independent adjustment, so that

I can have a perfectly horizontal marver even when the torch is tilted to direct the flame up at an angle. I also use a handheld marver that is about 1½ x 2½ inches (3.8 x 6.3 cm) wide. Mine is made of graphite, although many beadmakers use brass, which is helpful in bringing out the colors of silver laden glass.

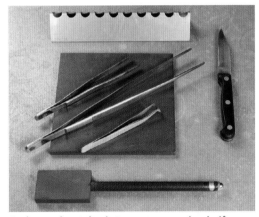

A glass rod rest, basic tweezers, a paring knife, a tabletop marver, and a handheld marver

My torch setup, with the different types of marvers I frequently rely on: tabletop, handheld, and torch-mounted

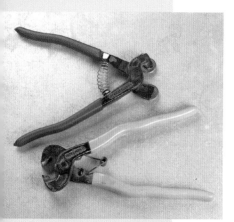

Disk cutters (at top) and tile cutters

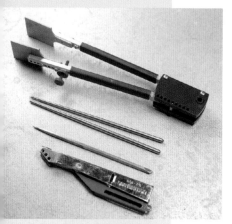

Barbecue-style mashers, steel chopsticks for punties, a steel pick, and a piezoelectric igniter

Glass cutters There are two basic types of cutters. *Tile cutters* were originally designed to cut tile and have two opposing sharp edges that come together in a straight cut. I prefer these for cutting rods of glass. *Disk cutters* have two disks with sharp edges that also work well for cutting glass. I prefer these for cutting pieces of murrini from a murrini cane. Both cutters work well. Which set you use depends on your personal preference.

Parallel mashers The early versions of these mashers were adapted from a barbeque tool. I like a masher that can be adjusted with a set screw, so it won't mash the bead too thin. The ideal masher has parallel surfaces, is comfortable in the hand, and squeezes easily without much resistance. Thick steel mashing surfaces mean that the tool won't overheat from contact with hot glass, which can cause the metal to deform.

Pick My steel pick is another handmade tool given me by Amnon Elbaz (he's a wizard with steel). One end is honed to a point; the other is shaped like a small dental spatula. Virtually any pick of steel or brass is handy to have on the bench. Ask your dentist to save used dental instruments for you, and you'll find a treasure trove of picks.

TORCHES

The project beads in this book were all created with a *dual-fuel*, surface-mix torch fueled by oxygen and propane. These torches are sometimes referred to as dual gas, which is probably a more accurate term. I think that some of the beads could also be made using a single-fuel torch, which typically consists of a torch head mounted on a gas canister, but I haven't tried it. (The Project Testers also used dual-fuel torches.) A single-fuel torch is limited by its inability to fine-tune the flame, so it will be frustrating to use in some of the tutorials. If that's all you have, try to keep your beads small and somewhat less complex.

After years of using a flint striker to light my torch, I now use a *piezoelectric igniter*, sold by welding-supply companies. Students find them far easier to use; they provide a spark every time the trigger is squeezed. I no longer teach students to light the flow of propane before adding oxygen (which is standard with flint). Oxygen is necessary for the igniter to work, so students are taught to turn on the oxygen a tiny bit, add propane, and then light the stream of gas with a spark from the igniter.

Beginners seem to encounter two easily correctible problems. They turn the igniter so the spark is facing away from them, and thus away from the flow of gas, which interferes with ignition. And sometimes they open the propane valve so far that a lot of gas is expelled. Then, of course, when the spark meets the gas, there's a big *whoosh!* of flame. The second problem is self-correcting. Once students are startled by that flame, they tend to be more careful the next time.

In my studio I have both tanked oxygen (purchased from a welding-supply company) and an oxygen concentrator. When I'm teaching and thus using a lot of gas, I work with two oxygen tanks that are connected to each other in series

A dual-fuel torch with torch-mounted marver

and then to a regulator, which I set at around 12 to 14 psi (83 to 97 kPa). Your own setting will depend on the torch you're using. I use the first tank until it's empty, then I close the valve on it and open the valve on the second tank.

When I'm working alone, without students or a torch buddy, I switch to the oxygen concentrator—a medical unit for patients who need a continuous supply of oxygen. This small unit doesn't require a regulator; your torch will use all the oxygen that a concentrator can supply. I don't find a significant difference in the different sources of oxygen, although some torches are better suited to low pressure than others. The advantage of the concentrator is that, in the long run, it's less expensive than tanked oxygen.

I purchase propane in tanks that have roughly double the capacity of barbecue-size tanks. My propane regulator is set at about 6 psi (41 kPa). Although my torch will also burn natural gas, I find that the propane flame is hotter, probably because I can increase the pressure. (The pressure of natural gas in my studio is controlled by the gas company, and it's very low.)

There are many torches on the market that are suitable for beadmaking. I like to use a torch with a highly adjustable flame that can range from big and bushy to pinpoint and tight. I prefer the ability to tilt the torch for certain tasks, and I want a torch to be as low maintenance as possible.

Glass rods ready for use

GLASS

The project beads in this book were made primarily with Italian soft glass (also called *soda-lime glass*) with a *coefficient of expansion* (or *COE*) of 104. The general rule is that all of the glass you combine in a single bead should have the same COE. Because glass types with different COEs expand and contract at different rates as they heat and cool, a mixed-glass bead will crack. Of course, as with any rule, this one has its exceptions; we'll address these as they occur in the tutorials.

Italian soft glass is readily available and comes in a wide variety of colors. There are no other rules, and you should feel free to use any brand or type of soft glass that interests you (or that you can get your hands on).

I generally use rods of glass that are 5 to 6 mm in diameter. If I'm encasing a bead in clear glass (such as the End-of-Day Bead on page 118), I prefer German glass because it's less prone to bubble in the flame or become sooty, but use whichever clear glass works best for you and your equipment.

Hint: If you find brown or gray streaks in the clear glass of a finished project, there is soot or dirt in your glass. Clean your rods thoroughly before using, work a little cooler, and slightly increase the oxygen in your gas mixture. All of these should eliminate the soot problem.

workshop*wisdom*

A few terms pop up regularly in the book. Here's what they mean.

Footprint A bead's footprint is the width of the space that it occupies on a mandrel.

Gather A gather is an accumulation of molten glass, which, thanks to the physical properties of glass, is naturally round. A *juicy gather* is so molten that it's almost white hot and very droopy.

Punty Traditionally, a punty is an iron rod used to handle molten glass. We've probably all seen images of glassworkers reaching into a furnace to retrieve glass on the end of a punty. In beadmaking, the term refers to any handle that permits us to hang on to a piece of glass. It could be another glass rod or a stainless steel chopstick.

Shocky The soft glass used for the beads in this book is sensitive to sudden and extreme changes in heat. A shocky bead is highly susceptible to fracturing when introduced to the heat of the flame.

9

WORK STATION

Everyone should work in a setting that's comfortable and safe. I work in a cushioned, office-style chair on wheels. Because the floor is concrete, the chair slides easily, so that I can grab glass or tools I've left out of reach and can push away from the table quickly if a bit of hot glass drops too close to my lap. (I can also rotate my chair to switch on, or adjust, my overhead ventilation.) There's a task lamp focused on my torch area, and as much natural light as possible.

My kiln is also close by, in case I need to access components I've garaged or insert finished beads for annealing. An assortment of mandrels that have been dipped in bead release are stored upright in sand-filled containers, and my most-used tools are on my bench. Alternative tools, or those that I'm not relying on at the moment, are in drawers just to one side.

On my work bench, natural light is supplemented by a task light.

Annealing

A great deal has been written on the subject of *annealing*—the controlled cooling of a bead to eliminate internal stress that would otherwise be present in the glass. As a result, some confusing and contradictory information has made its way into the brains of beadmakers. Absent annealing, internal stress leaves a glass bead perpetually unstable and prone to breakage. It might break today, next week, or never; you just don't know. And so, in order to ensure the integrity of your work, your beads must ultimately be annealed.

Annealing can't be done without a *kiln* (sometimes referred to as an oven), the temperature of which is monitored by a thermometer called a *pyrometer*, and it can't be done without slowly reducing the temperature over a period of several hours. This book assumes that you have a kiln nearby and can pop a hot bead into it as soon as you've completed it in the torch.

If you don't have ready access to a hot kiln, you can try to cool your beads in a *fiber blanket* or *vermiculite* until they reach room temperature. If they survive this cooling, they can be *batch annealed* later by putting a number of room-temperature beads into a cool kiln, slowly bringing it up to the annealing temperature for the glass being used, and then cooling it over several hours. Large beads (and some asym-

Annealing kiln with a "doggie door," in addition to a top lid

metrical beads) are difficult to cool successfully this way, because the relatively rapid decrease in temperature makes the bead more susceptible to thermal shock. If this is your only option, work small, encase the hot bead thoroughly in the blanket or vermiculite as soon as it has stopped glowing, and *don't* peek at the bead until it's completely cooled.

Some of the tutorial sessions will be easier if your kiln permits you to "garage" certain components until you need them. For example, the murrini for the End-of-Day Bead (page 118) and the Eye Bead (page 36) can be preheated in a kiln and then removed when it's time to add them to the bead. This isn't critical, but it will make the project a little easier.

The kiln in my studio has a little doggie-style door that allows me to insert hot beads into it without opening the lid. I set the kiln's controller to maintain a temperature of 965°F (518°C) until I've placed the last bead of the day in the kiln. Assuming that the last bead is a large, focal one, the kiln stays at 965°F (518°C) for one more hour. It then cools at a rate of 100°F (38°C) per hour until it reaches 400°F (204°C), at which point it shuts off automatically and slowly cools to room temperature.

Safety

We are all responsible for our own safety. Every day, we encounter situations that are made safe only by our knowledgeable and careful conduct. Before we drive a car, cross a street, or take a swim, we're careful to educate ourselves about the skills required.

Beadmaking, too, requires a set of safety skills. Beginners should take the time to obtain the information that will enable them to set up safe beadmaking studios and to work safely with glass and torches. Because this book is aimed at advanced beginners and intermediate students, I don't spend pages and pages on studio setup and safety. What follows is just a brief refresher, *not* a substitute for all the information beginners must acquire.

CLOTHING AND EYE PROTECTION

When you're ready to torch, tie back long hair and avoid shirts with dangling ties or billowing sleeves. Instead, choose close-fitting clothing that covers as much of your body as possible, ideally made of natural fibers that won't catch fire easily. In my chilly winter studio, I wear a long-sleeve, cotton T-shirt under a polyester fleece sweatshirt.

All beadmakers know that cold rods hurried into a hot flame will sometimes spit bits of glass. Bits that strike the fleece melt it and stick to it, but won't burn through to the cotton below. Although I practice what I preach, and usually remember to point the hot end of the rod at the work surface until it has started to melt, cotton and fleece give me protection from the inevitable shocky rod. (I treat myself to a new fleece every November.)

Beadmaking on a dual-fuel torch requires both eye protection (a heatproof lens between your eye and the glass and flame) and filtration (a lens that subtracts the sodium flare that is visible when soft glass melts). High-quality, comfortable eyewear is a great investment. The glasses last a long time and will cut down on eyestrain when you torch.

If, like me, you need a complicated prescription, consider getting prescription eyewear for the torch. Although it's possible to add a protective clip-on lens, combining them in one frame is the ultimate solution (though, alas, more expensive).

If you're in the habit of using magnifying lenses, look into the stick-on magnifiers that are made of a vinyl-like material.

VENTILATION AND RESPIRATORS

Adequate studio ventilation is a must. A torch is indiscriminate; it gobbles up not only the oxygen that is fed to it through a hose but also the oxygen in the room—the oxygen you were planning to inhale. Under ordinary circumstances, when you aren't using particularly

Prescription eyewear with flip-up, filtered lenses

dusty or noxious materials, you need a simple arrangement of an exhaust fan that will pull stale air out of the room and an open window or door that will supply fresh air. Good ventilation should pull fumes away from your face and out of your work area, and allow the air to be replaced continuously.

Good ventilation isn't a substitute for a respirator, which should always be worn when you work with dusts or particulates, such as enamels and reduction powders. You'll also need protection from the fumes that result from applying metals, such as copper, gold, silver, and palladium; purchase an appropriate cartridge respirator for these tasks. If you're handling only enamels and powders, an inexpensive particulate respirator (which looks a bit like a common dust mask) will do, but a cartridge respirator is your safest bet—one rated by NIOSH (the National Institute for Occupational Safety and Health)

A respirator with replaceable cartridges (at right) and a dust mask

My ergonomic work station, with armrests and elbow pads

as at least N-100. Keep in mind that dusty substances like enamels and crushed aventurine can become airborne; clean them up with damp paper towels, and dispose of the towels in closed containers.

STUDIO SETUP

For the safest possible working environment, the surfaces in your studio should be heatproof. Wooden tables can be temporarily covered with ceramic or stone tiles or sheets of steel. I enjoy a cement floor in my studio, but you can purchase fireproof fabrics to cover almost any type of floor. Cement board, ceramic tile, or stone tiles are excellent options for placing under and around a kiln. Remember that the kiln should be a safe distance from walls and other flammable surfaces. The wall behind my kiln is brick.

Your studio should be equipped with a fire extinguisher. Fire extinguishers expire, so check yours on a set schedule. And keep a bowl of water on your work surface. You'll need it for quenching tools and disposing of bits of hot glass, but in a pinch, it's also the first thing you could dump on an errant flame.

The hoses leading to your torch should be attached with quick disconnects; in the event of fire, these provide the fastest way to separate the supply of fuel from the torch—and thus stop fueling the flames. Quick disconnects are also handy if you own more than one torch, because they let you swap torches easily. Your torch should be clamped or bolted to the table so that you don't accidentally knock it onto the floor or into your lap. My torch is clamped with a large, C-shaped clamp that holds in place not only the torch but also the ergonomic station that I have begun to use around my torch. This setup allows me to have wrist and elbow rests that cut down on fatigue.

Tanks of oxygen must be secured so they can't be knocked over. If an oxygen tank is knocked to the ground and its valve dislodged, it becomes a missile, thanks to the pressurized gas that's expelled through the narrow hole at its top. A tank can be braced against or chained to a wall, or secured in a specialized base sold by gas-supply companies.

Oxygen tanks and concentrators can be stored indoors, but the safest place for propane tanks is outside. Even so-called leakproof tanks can leak, and propane is highly flammable. Although you might think you'd smell a gas leak before it became dangerous, because propane is heavier than air, it pools on the floor; by the time you smell it, you're at great risk. Propane tanks can be stored outdoors under as simple an arrangement as an overturned trash can, and can temporarily supply gas through a hose that passes through an open window or a hole in a wall.

How to Use This Book

This book consists of a series of tutorials organized as skill-building exercises for intermediate beadmakers. Each tutorial focuses on a single finished bead—the project bead—that serves to introduce the materials and techniques of that tutorial. There are step-by-step instructions and plenty of photos. I've tried to sprinkle each tutorial with words of bead wisdom, and hopefully I answer your questions as if we were in a classroom together.

One way to approach the project beads is to gather the materials and tools described in any given tutorial, and then attempt to copy the bead as a way of mastering the techniques that making it entails. In my classes, I usually encourage students to copy the bead I'm teaching, so that they're exposed to the process twice: first when they watch me at the torch, and again when they attempt the same maneuvers on their own. Here, your first exposure to a bead is in reading the tutorial. Your reinforcement is when you undertake to make the same bead.

Copy the bead if you find it challenging. If you don't want to (maybe it's too easy for you, or you don't like it), focus instead on whatever aspect of the tutorial is novel to you, and attempt to incorporate that aspect of the bead into your own work. Maybe it's a new use for a tool, a material you haven't encountered, or a different way to approach a familiar shape. Whatever information challenges you is what you can take away from that tutorial.

The last pages of each tutorial are devoted to the work of the Project Testers (page 5), followed by a gallery of beads by other artists. I have selected the gallery beads because they express some aspect of the skills and materials used in the tutorial. These are *not* beads to copy, but to study and enjoy—to see how an accomplished beadmaker turns building-block skills into expressions of art and creativity. True, these galleries are "eye candy," but they're also inspiration, because they show us what hard work, skill, and practice can achieve.

The online bead community is full of tutorials, most of which teach the reader how to make a particular bead identified with a particular artist. Both generous and efficient, these tutorials respond to requests from beginners and fellow beadmakers who want to understand the artist's individual style and technique.

Although the tutorials in this book are very similar to the ones online, there are some significant differences. Most important, the project beads were carefully developed to teach specific materials, tools, and methods. They're not beads that are identified personally with me. As I mentioned at the outset, these are building blocks, not the ultimate structure. After working through these teaching sessions, you should almost immediately be able to expand upon them, translate them, and transform them into your own work, *not* mine. If you think this is impossible, take a look at the Project Testers' pages. In their first attempts to follow the tutorials, many of those artists produced beads that soar far beyond the original project in energy and beauty.

We are all making beads, we are all using glass, and we are all human. Those are factors we have in common. The artistic energy and personal message of our beads are our individual fingerprints. Every bead made is unique to that artist. I hope that the skills you encounter in this book will enhance your own unique approach to glass beads and the works of art you ultimately produce.

Ruffled Pendant

This versatile pendant can be executed in many different color schemes, with results that range from a light and airy flower to an Asian-influenced fan or a realistic seashell.

What Will This Session Teach?

The primary challenge of this project is to manage the heat base of the glass so that the portion of the pendant that's distant from the mandrel remains stable and uncracked. You can enhance that challenge and gain additional skills by using gold leaf, a striking glass color, and ruffling pliers, as I did.

Glass & Materials
- Glass rods Ⓐ
    - Transparent light amethyst
    - Transparent medium amethyst
    - Gold pink (also called *rubino oro*)
- Gold leaf Ⓓ

Tools
- Basic hand tools (page 6)
- Baz Box Ⓑ
- Ruffling pliers Ⓒ
- Tweezer Ⓔ

Notes on Tools and Materials

Gold leaf Gold is a precious metal with a high melting point and superior malleability, which means it can be produced in microscopically thin sheets. The result is the rich metallic sheen of gold at a far lower cost than gold in its other forms.

Gold leaf typically comes in *books* of 25 *leaves*—sheets that are 3⅜ inches (8.6 cm) square. Leaf comes in two or three different weights; the heavier the leaf, the more expensive the book. For beadmaking, the lightest gold leaf gives as good a result as the heaviest. It's just a tad harder to use, because leaf tends to be very flyaway. The Baz Box (explained on the next page) helps with that problem.

> **workshop***wisdom*
>
> When pricing gold leaf, be careful to compare books of the same size and karat. When sellers refer to a *pack*, they are describing 20 books, or 500 leaves. Although that's way too much for beadmaking purposes, artisans who gild signs, artwork, or ceilings use far more, so they buy in bulk.

Gold leaf is available in different karats, ranging from 10 to 24 karat. The difference is the purity of the gold, with higher karats being purer and thus more intensely gold in color. Lower karat leaf looks more silvery. Most gold leaf sold for beadmaking is either 22 or 24 karat. I used 22 karat for the bead shown.

Baz Box Available from suppliers of beadmaking tools, a Baz Box is a 5 x 5-inch (12.7 x 12.7 cm) vacuum table designed to secure leaf or foil for use at the torch. The box has a gentle vacuum that sucks the leaf down against the flat, stainless steel top plate of the box through tiny holes.

For this project we'll use torn fragments of leaf that will rest on the Baz Box until needed. If we were using an entire sheet at a time, the box would handle that, too. It comes with a steel cover that holds down the unneeded portion of the gold leaf sheet so that it can be cleanly torn away when you touch the hot glass down on the desired portion of leaf (photo 1).

Ruffling pliers Sold as wire-bending pliers, these come in a variety of sizes and are designed for creating wire loops. One side of the pliers' jaw is round, and the other side is con-

cave or flat. These work beautifully to crease and ruffle glass, and they are one of my indispensable tools for fish fins, flower petals, and seashells (photo 2). Equally satisfying results can be had from pointed, unserrated tweezers, and some might even enjoy the imprint left by the serrated jaws.

An Overview

Although it's a simple form, this pendant presents the challenge of maintaining a large mass of glass at a distance from the core heat provided by the mandrel. In this coloration, the gold leaf on the ruffled pendant bead shimmers. This bead poses equally beautifully as a fan, an ivory seashell, or a delicate flower.

Creating the Bead
PREPARING THE GOLD LEAF

Cut off about a third of a sheet of gold leaf, rip it into three or four irregular fragments, and lay them on top of the box, in easy reach of the torch (photo 3). Then turn on the box.

workshop*wisdom*

Gold leaf isn't easy to handle with bare fingers, so make use of the special papers that come between the leaves of the book. Tear the sheet while it's sandwiched between two pieces of the paper, then remove one piece of paper and, using the other to hold the sheet, put the leaf on top of the box (photo 4).

MAKING THE BASE BEAD

This bead begins with a tube of transparent medium amethyst approximately ¾ inch (1.9 cm) long. The tube's diameter should be three times the diameter of the mandrel, to make certain the bead won't be too shocky or lack structural integrity.

One way to create a tube with evenly puckered holes is to lay down two spacer beads that will become the ends of the tube (photo 5). Next, coil glass onto the mandrel in between the two spacer beads. Warm the coiled glass, and roll it on a handheld marver to shape it into a tube (photos 6 and 7). Be careful not to overheat the ends of the bead or they'll draw into the center, and the ends will be sharp and pointy. Instead, introduce the most heat to the center of the tube. The radiant heat from the bead will keep the ends warm but leave them in place, maintaining the puckered holes.

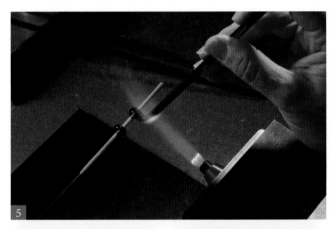

ADDING THE RUFFLE

The body of the ruffle is constructed of concentric rings of glass, alternating between the transparent light amethyst and the gold pink. The first coil of glass is the light amethyst; place it in a semicircle that begins and ends at the center of the tube. Essentially, this semicircle is like a capital letter C on one side of the tube. The opening in the C serves as the front of the pendant (photo 8).

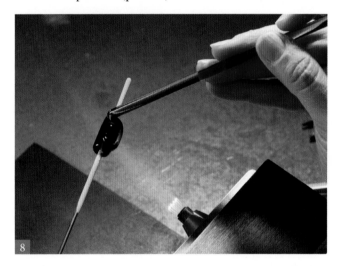

Palladium leaf on this aqua ruffle reinforces the cool blue color scheme

17

The next coil of glass is gold pink applied slightly outside the footprint of the first coil. That's because the wraps of glass will get wider and wider, to create the ruffle of the bead, which is wider than the base bead. This second C has a wider opening in the front (photo 9). Continue adding coils, alternating colors, until you have four coils, each applied to a slightly wider C (photo 10). Then add one more coil of glass at the bottom of the ruffle.

While adding the coils of glass, it's important to flash the base bead in and out of the flame periodically, to keep it warm and prevent it from cracking. The base bead doesn't need to be glowing hot; just keep it warm, which won't change its shape in any way. The challenge is to keep the base and the ruffle warm without introducing so much heat that the ruffle collapses. Because the ruffle extends away from the mandrel, it has a tendency to lose heat quickly.

workshop*wisdom*

One of the frequent problems students encounter is that the coils of glass don't adequately adhere to each other, and the bead shocks apart or breaks between the rings. This happens when the glass has a *cold connection*—meaning that the hot glass was applied to glass that was too cold, and the two didn't join properly. To make sure the hot coils that you're adding attach to the bead properly, prewarm the bead and apply extra heat to the surface where you intend to add the glass.

APPLYING THE LEAF

Gold leaf adheres easily to warm glass and, once adhered, it won't burn away in the flame necessary to ruffle the glass with the pliers. On the other hand, leaf that's not adhered to glass will burn easily, and it's a lot harder to attach the leaf after the pendant is ruffled. So the next step is applying the fragments of gold leaf to the bead.

Warm the area where you want to apply the leaf. Then, holding the bead just outside the flame, use pointy tweezers to pick up a piece of gold leaf and place it on the bead (photo 11). Immediately use the side of the tweezers to burnish the leaf onto the bead, then return it to the flame. When you heat the leaf, it will get shiny and taut where it's adhered to the surface. You can then move on to apply leaf to other spots. Try to overdo it a little, because a small portion of the leaf might burn away in the ruffling step that comes next.

If you have trouble grabbing on to the gold leaf with the tweezers, try heating a spot on the bead and touching that spot to the leaf. The Baz Box surface is heatproof, so hot glass won't harm it (photo 12).

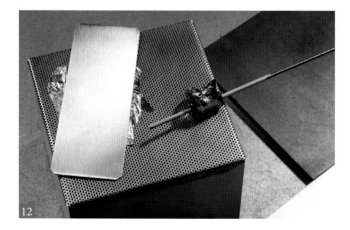

RUFFLING

Before ruffling, remember to heat the base bead, so that heat builds up in that part of the bead and keeps it stable while you work elsewhere.

Starting in the center of the ruffle, heat the ruffle and pinch it with the pliers or pointy tweezers (photo 13). Usually, I heat and then pinch about three times before the glass loses its malleability. To pinch the glass and get it to ruffle, it must be hot enough to move when pressed in the jaws of the pliers—which means it will be glowing—but it doesn't need to be red hot. If the glass is too hot, it will slump onto the tube, or maybe onto the table, before you can pinch it in the pliers. On the other hand, if you're trying to ruffle glass that's too cold, you'll hear a crunch as you pinch, meaning you're cracking cold glass. If that happens, try to reheat and repair where you've cracked the ruffle.

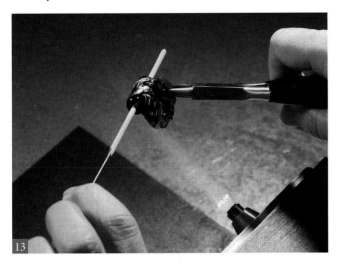

Pinching about three times after each reheating, move around the entire ruffle until its appearance pleases you. I usually hold the pliers in one consistent position, keeping the concave side of the jaws on the interior of the ruffle. Other effects can be achieved by changing the pliers' position, or by alternating pliers and tweezers. This part should be fun.

The gold pink glass is a striking color (see Workshop Wisdom below), so there's one last essential step. After the entire bead is ruffled and you're pleased with its shape, gently reheat the entire ruffle everywhere you've used the gold pink glass, so it will strike to its deep gold pink color (photo 14). Sometimes this is barely necessary, because the glass has been heated and cooled during the ruffling. Other times, you can see the nearly transparent gold pink glass strike in that final reheat. It has a lot to do with the particular batch of glass.

Many other design options work for this bead. Changing the colors of the glass—or using silver or palladium leaf—gives great results. Another approach is to turn the orientation of the bead to make a shell. For the shell here, I hand mixed transparent medium amber with light ivory and used that striated rod to create the bead (photo 15).

workshop*wisdom*

A striking color of glass is one that blushes to its full color potential after one or more cycles of heating, cooling, and reheating. This is relatively straightforward in most of the Italian glasses, with striking colors that include transparent orange, red, and yellow. More recently, many silver laden colors have come on the market; they also require striking to bring out their full palette. These can be trickier, and require familiarity with the particular type of glass to understand the necessary cycle of heating and cooling.

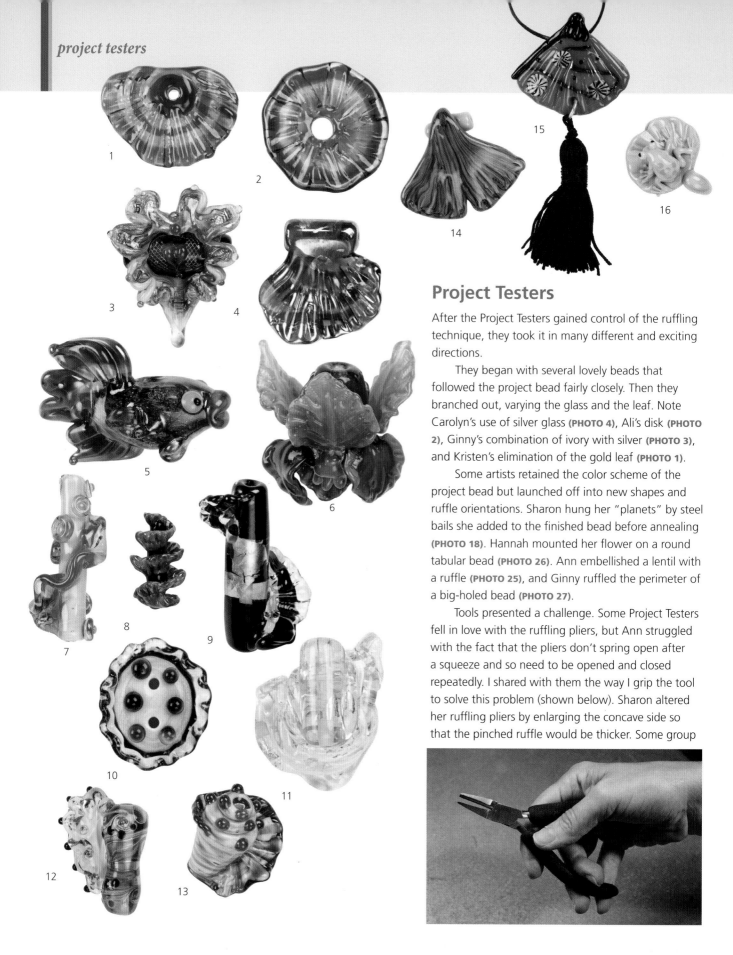

1

2

3

5

4

14

15

16

6

7

8

9

10

11

12

13

Project Testers

After the Project Testers gained control of the ruffling technique, they took it in many different and exciting directions.

They began with several lovely beads that followed the project bead fairly closely. Then they branched out, varying the glass and the leaf. Note Carolyn's use of silver glass **(PHOTO 4)**, Ali's disk **(PHOTO 2)**, Ginny's combination of ivory with silver **(PHOTO 3)**, and Kristen's elimination of the gold leaf **(PHOTO 1)**.

Some artists retained the color scheme of the project bead but launched off into new shapes and ruffle orientations. Sharon hung her "planets" by steel bails she added to the finished bead before annealing **(PHOTO 18)**. Hannah mounted her flower on a round tabular bead **(PHOTO 26)**. Ann embellished a lentil with a ruffle **(PHOTO 25)**, and Ginny ruffled the perimeter of a big-holed bead **(PHOTO 27)**.

Tools presented a challenge. Some Project Testers fell in love with the ruffling pliers, but Ann struggled with the fact that the pliers don't spring open after a squeeze and so need to be opened and closed repeatedly. I shared with them the way I grip the tool to solve this problem (shown below). Sharon altered her ruffling pliers by enlarging the concave side so that the pinched ruffle would be thicker. Some group

17

18

19

members used tweezers or dental tools to achieve the ruffled effect.

Ultimately, most of the group explored the ruffle in fun and innovative ways—for example, the spiraling ruffles by Emma **(PHOTO 8)**, Ann **(PHOTO 9)**, and Debby **(PHOTO 7)**. Ruffles lend themselves to seashell shapes, such as the beads from Hannah **(PHOTO 13)**, Wendy **(PHOTO 12)**, and Hayley **(PHOTO 22)**. Wendy's button **(PHOTO 10)** and Jackie's clear ruffle with gold leaf **(PHOTO 11)** show how ruffling transparent glass makes it more reflective.

Jen presented the group with ruffled butterflies **(PHOTOS 23 AND 24)**. Inspired by a gathering of the International Society of Glass Beadmakers in Florida, Sharon created her joyous *Elton in Miami* **(PHOTO 20)**.

Several group members successfully incorporated ruffles in their existing body of work, as in Carolyn's fish **(PHOTO 5)** and Hannah's elegant irises **(PHOTO 6)**. Wendy claimed that this project was difficult for her, but her graceful white lily belies that **(PHOTO 21)**.

The versatility of the ruffling technique is clear from the jewelry created by Emma and Hannah. Emma's boisterous choker is constructed on colored craft wire **(PHOTO 19)**. Hannah's seed bead necklace includes her ruffle bead as the centerpiece within similarly hued crystals **(PHOTO 17)**. Sylvie's pendants introduce an Asian feel **(PHOTOS 14, 15, AND 16)**.

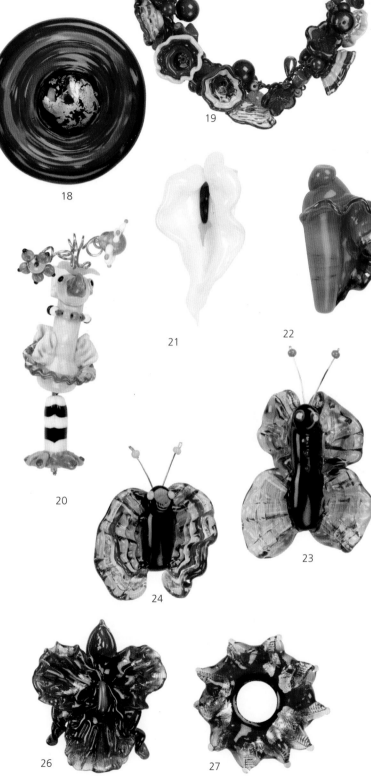

21

22

20

24

23

25

26

27

gallery

Ann Scherm Baldwin
Atlantis, 2009
2⅛ x 1⅞ x ¾ inches (5.5 x 4.5 x 2 cm)
Soft glass, dichro; ruffled lampwork
Photo by David L. Totten

Ofilia Cinta
Pink Hollow Lampwork Fish, 2009
2 x 3¾ x 1⅝ inches (5 x 9.5 x 4 cm)
Soft glass
Photo by artist

Karen Leonardo
Ruffled Flower Garden, 2010
  *Blue Rust Flowe*r (top left), 1⅞ x 1⅜ x 2 inches (4.5 x 3.5 x 5 cm);
  Scarlet Flower (right), 2⅛ x 1⅛ x 2 inches (5.5 x 3 x 5 cm);
  Patina Blue Primrose (bottom left), 2⅛ x 1⅛ x 2 inches (5.5 x 3 x 5 cm)
Boro; flameworked
Photo by artist

Ann Scherm Baldwin
Snookums, 2009
2¾ x 2 x ¾ inches (7 x 5 x 2 cm)
Soft glass, dichro; ruffled lampwork
Photo by David L. Totten

Jiley
Mask Bead, 2008
2 x 1⅝ inches (5 x 4 cm)
Soft glass
Photo by artist

Sara Sally LaGrand
Geneviève, 2010
3 x 5 x 1 inches (7.6 x 12.7 x 2.5 cm)
Soft glass, wire wrap; lampworked
Photo by artist

Susan "Meow Meow" Pack
Untitled, 2009
2¼ x 1⅞ x 1⅜ inches (5.6 x 4.8 x 3.5 cm)
Soft glass; lampworked
Photo by artist

Karen Leonardo
Scarlett Ruffled Bloom, 2010
2⅛ x 1⅛ x 2 inches (5.5 x 3 x 5 cm)
Boro; flameworked
Photo by artist

Cheery Little Guy

An eye-catching focal piece when worn alone on a neck wire, this little guy makes a fabulously amusing group when strung with several of his buddies.

What Will This Session Teach?

This bead builds on the heat-control skills practiced on the Ruffled Pendant in Session 1. Once again, you'll work on maintaining an adequate heat base in the part of the bead that's distant from the mandrel. The challenge is greater this time. You'll maneuver the glass with shaping tools, move the bead around the flame as you work on the hair, and add cooler bits of glass for the eyes, mouth, and hair.

Glass & Materials

Glass rods Ⓐ
>	Opaque red
>	Transparent medium aqua
>	Opaque yellow
>	Opaque white

Bull's-eye-patterned murrini cane Ⓓ

Frit, blue and green, small Ⓕ

Clear micro beads, 1–2 mm in diameter Ⓔ

Tools

Basic hand tools (page 6)

Grooved marver Ⓑ

Pin punch, ³⁄₁₆ inch (5 mm) in diameter Ⓒ

Notes on Tools and Materials

Murrini These are slices cut from a bundle of glass rods that have been fused together and then pulled to a smaller diameter. Each slice yields an image or pattern within its cross section, in the same way that slices of a jellyroll reveal a spiral (photo 1). The cane for the pupil of the Eye Bead (Session 3) is a simple murrini. Session 10, the End-of-Day Bead, uses commercial, presliced murrini.

For this bead, the murrini are cut with tile nippers from an entire rod of the same pattern. Many murrini vendors will sell the rods even though they don't typically offer them for sale in catalogs or on the Internet; just ask. By cutting the murrini myself, I can make precise slices about ⅛ inch (3 mm) thick. For my bead, the murrini's colors—from the center to the outer ring of the bulls-eye—are green, dark blue, mustard, brown, white, and blue (photo 2).

Frit The speckled finish in the little guy's hair is made from finely chopped or crushed glass, called *frit*. Different suppliers describe frit size differently, but for this bead you'll want fine or small frit, just one step coarser than what is usually sold as *powder*.

Frit is commercially available from many different suppliers, some of whom also sell color mixtures that they've prepared. Frit is usually *not* 104 COE, but despite the classic wisdom that you should never combine glass of different COEs, here

workshop*wisdom*

If you already have sliced murrini on hand, you can grind them to a uniform thickness on a flat lap grinder or other diamond-grinding surface. To handle such a tiny piece of glass, wear a latex glove and use one finger to press down on the murrini while the wheel spins. The glove provides better traction for hanging on to the murrini. A simple, flat, diamond-coated paddle, used to dress bead holes, also works. Be sure to keep the grinding surface wet as you work (photo 3).

the rules can be bent—if you're careful. Small amounts of incompatible frit won't usually compromise the integrity of a bead. Don't overdo it, though, and if the bead cracks, consider frit as the possible culprit.

If you want frit that's 100 percent compatible with the COE of the glass you're using, consider making your own. For this bead, I made my frit using a commercially available set of frit crusher and screens (photo 4). (Just follow the manufacturer's instructions.) Not only is it easy to do, but it's also an excellent way to use up scraps and make the palette of your beads truly unique. Just remember that certain colors of glass react with each other (for example, turquoise and ivory). Too much reactive glass in your frit will give you a muddy mess.

Micro beads Available from frit and glass suppliers, these tiny glass globes aren't technically beads, because they're not pierced with a hole. They're used for crafting and scrapbooking projects, usually stuck to double-sided tape. Although micro beads are of an uncertain COE (see page 9 for a discussion of *coefficient of expansion*, or COE), they don't seem problematic on the surface of 104 COE glass, the type used in this bead. If you can't find micro beads, little dots of clear glass applied from a skinny stringer will give the same dimensional effect.

Grooved marver Typically made of steel or brass, a grooved marver has a surface of channels (or grooves), which produce a grooved surface in the glass.

Pin punch I first saw this tool when I watched bead artist Sharon Peters use it in a demonstration. I found a set in all different sizes in a hardware store. Sharon used it in the process of making eyes in her creatures, but I use my pin punch to form the mouth of the guy.

An Overview

In my version of this bead, the guy has a spunky attitude, with a smirk and a sideways glance. Playing with the angle of the features or the color of the eyes or hair can produce a full cast of intriguing little characters.

Creating the Bead

Before lighting the torch, make sure you have the components near at hand, and that you've cut a few extra murrini slices, just in case. I like to rest the murrini on the torch-mounted marver so they're prewarmed, but they can be shocky whatever you do, and if one breaks as you apply it to a bead, it's nearly impossible to cut another one while keeping your bead warm in the torch. Frit and micro beads are also tricky to manipulate while keeping the bead warm, which is why I like to have them close by before starting.

MAKING THE BASE

Wind on the opaque yellow glass into a fat tube about 1 inch (2.5 cm) wide and ½ inch (1.3 cm) in diameter (photo 5). Add more yellow glass along the lower half of the tube, where the nose and mouth will appear (photos 6 and 7). (At this stage, the face is symmetrical and looks like an upside-down

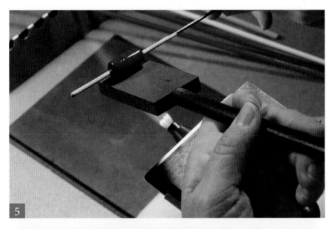

triangle. Although the chin is angled on my finished bead, that angle developed when I added the mouth [photo 8].)

Gently mash the tube and the extra glass that you've added so the head is now a thick wafer at least three times the diameter of the mandrel (photo 9). The shape should still resemble an upside-down triangle, although the chin area could be a blunted triangle tip.

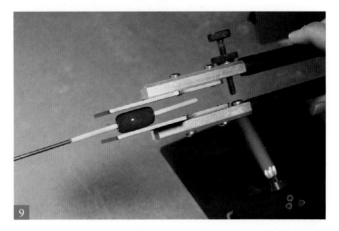

When flattening a bead, its final thickness should never be less than three times the diameter of the mandrel, or the bead might crack. To make a flatter or thinner bead, use a mandrel of a smaller diameter. In the end, the goal is always a wall of glass the thickness of the mandrel, on either side of the bead hole.

FIXING THE HAIR

Next, use the transparent aqua glass to stripe on hair. To do this, create a juicy gather at the end of the glass rod, pre-warm the top of the head, and then paint on a stripe of glass from that gather, running from the far left of the head to the far right. Repeat at least three times.

There are many ways to stripe on the glass for the hair. One method is to hold the mandrel virtually parallel to the flame, and pass the rod of glass through the flame (photo 10). Then, holding the glass rod in one spot, where it's red hot, touch the head at one end and move the head so that the glass stripes to the other end, using the flame to burn through the gather, and disconnect. Using hot glass this way causes it to flow down onto the head a little bit. When you look at the head, that front strip of aqua has a greenish tint, because you're looking at the transparent glass over the opaque yellow.

Another method is to create the gather in the flame, but hold the mandrel at right angles to the flame and just below it (photo 11). Again, the gather is striped from left to right, and when it's just beyond one side of the head, it's disconnected by burning through the glass with the flame. Remember to keep the entire head warm while you're working on the hair.

Now heat the aqua hair until it glows red, and roll it on the grooved marver. *Don't* press it down. Instead, rest the face of the bead on the marver and then *roll* it on its hair until the back of the head is on the marver (photo 12). I start with the face down so that any excess glass presses further down the back of the head. Even if the grooves aren't precise, wait to refine them until the rest of the face is complete. Focusing your energies on different areas of the face helps ensure that no part of the bead gets dangerously cool.

OPENING THE EYES

To add the eyes, pick up a slice of murrini in serrated tweezers, holding it near the top third, and waving the bottom third (which will be the underside of the eye) in the back of the flame to gently warm it (photo 13). The trick is to get the bottom of the murrini hot enough that it won't be shocked when it contacts the hot face. Keeping the murrini warm in the flame, direct the flame at a spot on the face where one eye belongs until that spot glows (photo 14). Then quickly rest the back of the bead on the torch-mounted marver and press the murrini into the head at that glowing spot (photo 15). Don't tweak that eye yet; go ahead and heat and insert the second murrini slice for the second eye (photo 16).

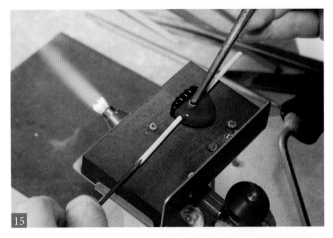

To press the murrini eyes farther into the head, use repeated applications of heat and pressing with mashers or a handheld marver (photo 17). By heating and pressing, you can overcome the murrini's tendency to draw inward. If the eyes protrude too far from the head, direct the heat at the face around the perimeter of the murrini and press it with the marver.

workshop*wisdom*

It's easier to start with murrini that don't have too much white in the pattern, because commercial murrini include a white glass that has a tendency to foam and become unsightly.

29

So far, the head has been symmetrical, but once you add the eyes, the little guy usually seems to be glancing to one side or another, developing some character. In my bead, he seems to be turning or glancing to *his* right, because his left eye was a little more prominent and both eyes were slightly to the right of center on his face.

ADDING THE MOUTH AND EAR

To add the mouth, place a large red dot in the lower half of the face, below and between the eyes (photo 18). Heat and flatten the dot with the marver until it's flush with the face (photo 19). Then add a slightly smaller white dot in the middle of the red dot (photo 20), and heat and flatten that dot with the marver.

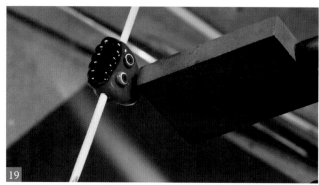

To make the mouth a perfect O shape, heat the white dot and plunge it deeper into the face, using the pin punch (photo 21). This usually also shapes the chin, but if the chin isn't large enough or angled enough, add more yellow or shape it with the marver.

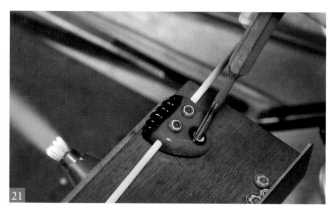

Angling the mouth will accentuate the feeling that he's looking to one side. To create the angle, heat one side of the mouth at about 2 o'clock. Then touch that heated spot with the tip of the red glass rod, and pull it slightly off to the side and up toward where the ear belongs (photo 22). Blow on the rod where it's attached to the mouth to cool it, and then snap it left to right to break it free. Use a little heat to smooth any nub of glass left behind.

More members of the Cheery Guy's Family

When a head is slightly turned, only one ear becomes visible. Because my guy is looking to his right, I heated the side of the head near his left eye and used a wedge-shaped steel pick to press in the illusion of an ear (photo 23).

Once you're happy with the eyes, mouth, and ear (or ears), remember to keep that part of the head warm while you return to finish the hair.

ADDING FRIT AND MICRO BEADS

Reheat the hair so it just starts to glow, and roll it in the frit (photos 24 and 25). This might take a couple of applications. The goal is to get the frit to stick to the glass but remain textured, so you don't want to melt the hair and frit together. If you do that, both the color and the texture of the frit will be lost.

Reheat the hair again, and use a knife or other tool to more deeply carve the crevices left by the grooved marver and make them more distinct (photo 26). This is necessary because the heating and addition of the frit tends to soften or distort the grooves.

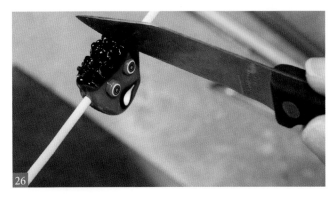

When you're happy with the frit, heat a particular spot and press it onto the micro beads (photo 27). Don't be surprised if the beads don't stick to the hot glass at first. It takes a little practice to get the glass the right temperature. Add a few micro beads here and there, or add a few dots of clear glass (photo 28). Give the bead one last reheating, and pop it in the kiln.

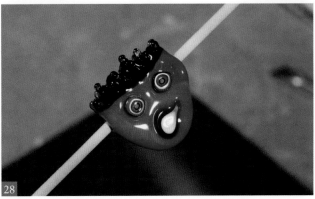

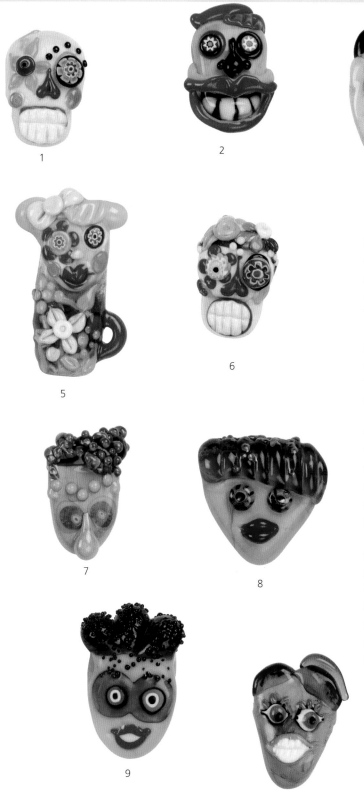

1

2

3

4

5

6

7

8

9

10

11

12

Project Testers

Not everyone in the group agreed that these beads were "cheery," regardless of the project title. As Ann said, "We're all very different personalities." That certainly helps explain why the resulting beads range from silly to sinister.

In designing this project, I thought the true challenge would be the off-center hole in the pendant causing havoc with the heat base of the bead. It turns out that no one struggled with that, but virtually everyone struggled with the murrini eyes.

Some avoided the murrini entirely by using dots for eyes. Dots arguably give more color control, but the trade-off is the loss of a certain whimsy. Jen **(PHOTO 23)**, Ann **(PHOTO 10)**, and Wendy **(PHOTO 15)** made expressive dot eyes. Sylvie used a combination of murrini and dots to produce a quirky look **(PHOTOS 22 AND 24)**.

Carolyn resorted to what she calls the "plunge-the-whole-cane-and-snap-it-off technique." She made her own murrini cane about 2 mm in diameter. When the "eye socket" was hot, Carolyn plunged in her rod, and then snapped it off, leaving a slice of murrini behind **(PHOTOS 20 AND 21)**. Of course, the fatter the cane, the more difficult the snap. Nippers might be required.

Sharon struggled with the murrini at first, but after encasing her finger in masking tape in lieu of a latex glove, she ground the murrini flat and had no problem creating the eyes. Her family's eyes are all commercial murrini **(PHOTOS 1, 2, 5, AND 6)**.

Personalities emerged from all the beads—for example, Emma's pirate and one-eyed girl with pigtails **(PHOTOS 18 AND 19)**. The mustache on Ann's guy **(PHOTO 3)** and the festive hat on Jen's party girl **(PHOTO 4)** suggest stories that are unfolding. Several Project Testers felt that each bead was just one member of a larger family, or one player in an as yet unwritten play. Emma plans to create a bird and crew for her pirate.

In addition to expressive murrini eyes, Project Testers played with hair. Note the wild hairstyles on Hayley's **(PHOTO 8)** and Debby's beads **(PHOTOS 7 AND 9)**. And Wendy made her little faces distinctively female by adding wispy tendrils and bangs **(PHOTOS 16 AND 17)**.

14

13

15

16

17

18

19

20

21

22

23

24

Jen Place, **13**; Ann Conlin, **14**; Carolyn Martin, **11**, **12**

Laurie Ament
Lalala, I Can't Hear You!, 2010
1 x 1⅛ x ⅜ inches (2.5 x 3 x 0.9 cm)
Soft glass; flameworked, raked, shaped,
      plunged, dotted
Photo by artist

Janice Peacock
Ancient South American Masks, 2009
Left, 1⅝ x 1⅜ x ¾ inches (4 x 3.5 x 2 cm); right, 2 x 1⅜ x ¾ inches (5 x 3.5 x 2 cm)
Soft glass, reduction powder, enamel; flameworked
Photo by artist

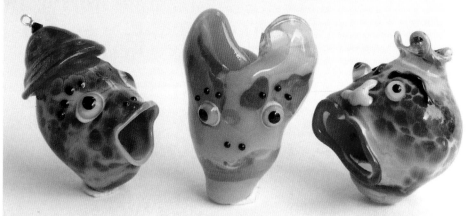

Robyn Keller Elbaz
Gossip, 2009–2010
Left to right, 2 x 1⅛ x 1⅜ inches (5 x 2.9 x 3.53 cm);
      2¼ x 1½ x 1⅜ inches (5.7 x 3.8 x 3.4 cm);
      2¼ x 1⅜ x 1⅝ inches (5.6 x 3.6 x 4.3 cm)
Soft glass, hollow-blown beads; flameworked
Photo by artist

Sharon Peters
Screaming Crab Pendant, 2008
15¾ x 15¾ x 6 inches
      (40 x 40 x 15 cm)
Soft glass, cabochon, silver bezel;
      flameworked
Photo by Jim Trenkle

Claudia Trimbur-Pagel
Gone with the Wind, 2009
1¼ x ½ inches (3.1 x 1.3 cm)
Soft glass, murrini
Photo by artist

Cathy A. Lybarger
Untitled, 2007
Left to right, 1⅞ x 1⅝ x ⅝ inches (4.8 x 4 x 1.5 cm);
   2⅛ x 1 x ⅞ inches (5.5 x 2.7 x 2.2 cm);
   2 x 1⅜ x ½ inches (5.2 x 3.5 x 1.4 cm)
Soft glass, hand-pulled eye murrini; flameworked
Photo by Jim Wildman

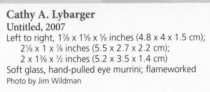

Susan Lambert
Sugar Skull, 2010
1 x 1 x ⅜ inches (2.5 x 2.5 x 1 cm)
Soft glass
Photo by artist

Jiley
Faces, 2010
Left to right, 1⅝ x ¾ inch (4 x 2 cm); 1⅜ x ⅝ inches (3.5 x 1.8 cm);
   1⅛ x ¾ inches (3 x 2 cm)
Soft glass
Photo by artist

In many cultures eye beads are worn
to ward off danger—say, the evil eye
from an enemy. The tabular shape
of this bead makes it equally suited
for a necklace pendant or a cuff-
style bracelet.

What Will This Session Teach?

This bead is all about reactions—aventurine reacting with enamel, reduction frit with silver. After you have demystified these reactions and learned how to make the murrini for the eye, you'll be able to use these same skills in many other bead styles, such as abstracts and florals.

Glass & Materials

Glass rods Ⓐ
- Transparent light amber
- Transparent light teal
- Intense black stringer, about 2 mm
- Transparent black, 2 rods

Iris gold reduction frit, small Ⓓ

Gold aventurine frit, small Ⓕ Ⓖ

Silver foil Ⓒ

Enamel, white Ⓔ

Tools

Basic hand tools (page 6)

Baz Box (page 16)

Stainless steel chopsticks Ⓑ

Notes on Tools and Materials

Intense black stringer In the Italian glass palette, black is actually a transparent color, made of very saturated purple glass. This can cause confusion when shopping in a glass catalog, because most colorists certainly don't look for black in the "transparent" category. Transparent black is usable when layered over an opaque that prevents light transmission, but when thinly applied, it looks purple. To remedy this problem, the manufacturers developed *intense black*, a black glass that is truly opaque. Its one drawback is its expense. Typically, I buy it as 2 or 3 mm stringers, which are more economical. This bead takes advantage of the properties of both intense black and transparent black.

Iris gold reduction frit This frit is made from *reduction glass*—glass that's formulated with large amounts of metals relative to typical glass recipes. In a neutral flame, where the oxygen and propane are balanced, the glass acts pretty much like all other glass. When exposed to a reducing flame—one with an excess of propane (or natural gas), which is to say a flame starved for oxygen—the metal oxides come to the surface and have some sort of reaction. The reaction is usually either a variegation of the color of the glass, or a shiny metallic exterior skin that forms on the surface. Here,

we're not relying on the frit's reduction properties but on its reactivity with silver. Mildly unpredictable, reduction glass is fun to work with.

Gold aventurine frit A more commonplace name for gold aventurine is *goldstone*, but the term *aventurine* is commonly used in the glass world, probably because it's derived from the Italian word for this material. Used extensively in traditional Venetian-style beads, aventurine is actually glass with suspended copper flecks or shavings that glitter like gold. It's also available in other colors, frequently sold as either blue or green aventurine.

Silver foil Both *leaf* and *foil* are very thin, delicate leaves of almost pure silver, also called *fine silver*. Leaf is thinner and thus slightly less expensive. The problem with leaf is that it can be very flyaway and hard to control. (See the discussion of a Baz Box to control gold leaf, page 16.) Silver foil is almost five times thicker than leaf, so although it's as thin as a light piece of paper, it can be carefully handled and shaped without disintegrating.

Enamels The available palette of enamel colors can be used to vary and expand the usual palette of glass. Sold in powdered form, enamels can be kneaded into a molten glass rod or sifted onto a glass surface, then encased or left exposed. It's important to use enamels that are compatible with your glass. For this project, which uses 104 COE glass, we're using a line of enamels that has been formulated specifically for that COE. (See page 9 for a discussion of COE, or coefficient of expansion.) It's unhealthy to inhale enamel dust, so take a moment to review the section on using particulates safely (page 12). At a minimum, wear a dust mask and use damp paper towels to clean up any spills.

workshop*wisdom*

The silver foil used here has a weight of about 160 grams for 1,000 sheets, and it's available in books of 25 leaves 3⅜ inches (8.6 cm) square. Knowing the weight is handy when shopping from catalogs or online, because the terminology varies.

Some sellers use the term foil for a 2-inch (5.1 cm)-wide strip of silver that's so heavy it can't be torn by hand (you'd need scissors or a punch). Sometimes what I am calling *foil* is called *heavy leaf*. Bottom line: If you see foil that's sold in a book of 25 leaves at a middle-tier price (leaf being cheaper and true foil being most expensive), you probably have the right stuff!

An Overview

No one seems to be neutral about eye beads. Many people collect them and view them as protective amulets; others find them off-putting, especially if they're too realistic. This bead couches the eye in a background that can appear as mystical or inexplicable as the eye itself.

Creating the Bead
PULLING THE STRINGER

On the end of a transparent black glass rod, pull a short stringer that remains attached to the rod. The stringer should be 1 to 2 mm in diameter and no more than 2 inches (5.1 cm) long. You'll use this stringer to rake the corners of the eye.

More specifically, heat a small gather at the end of the black rod, and pull the short stringer with tweezers as shown here. Or, warm the end of a second rod (any color you have handy is fine) in your other hand. When the gather is glowing, come out of the flame and touch the warm rod to the glowing gather. Pull the stringer when the glow has entirely subsided and the glass has gotten stiff, to make a thick stringer. Use a nipper to detach the pulling rod of glass, leaving a blunt end on the fat stringer (photos 1 and 2).

MAKING THE MURRINI CANE FOR THE PUPIL

In Session 2, Cheery Little Guy, we cut murrini from a purchased cane (see page 26). For this bead, we'll make our own cane and cut the murrini slices from it. I encourage you to experiment with this cane. Vary the types of frit, using reduction frits and plain glass frits. Try it with silver foil (as we do here), with silver leaf, and with no metals at all.

The cane begins with a thick cylinder of transparent amber about ¾ inch (1.9 cm) long. If you happen to have a rod 8 or 9 mm in diameter, that will work very well, but 4 to 5 mm is the norm. To create a thick cylinder at the end of a normal (thinner) rod, warm the end of the rod, and then heat it about 1 inch (2.5 cm) in from the end, until you're able to bend the rod against itself, essentially creating a doubled length of glass (photo 3). If that isn't thick enough, bend and fold the rod one more time, to create a triple thickness. Heat and shape this tripled glass to create the cylinder. Use the mashers to help achieve the cylinder shape, and also to make sure that all the air is squeezed out from the folds of glass, to avoid air bubbles in the final cylinder (photo 4). To keep a stiff handle on this heavy cylinder of glass, be sure to keep the flame on the cylinder, and not on the single thickness of the rod. The end of the cylinder should be blunt, not rounded—a result you can achieve by pressing it on a flat surface; here, my mashers were handy (photo 5).

Bring the outer surface of the cylinder to a dull glow, and roll it in the reduction frit several times. The idea is to get a thick coating, which at this stage will obscure the amber (photo 6). If necessary, reheat the cylinder and re-apply the frit a few times.

After the frit is applied, heat the surface of the cylinder again, and roll it on your marver to smooth the outer surface. Next, return the cylinder to a glow and roll up the silver foil onto the cylinder, with the help of your trusty Baz Box (photo 7). Use the side of a pair of tweezers or other metal tool to rub the silver onto the glass; this is called *burnishing* the silver (photo 8). Burnishing encourages the silver to melt onto the surface of the cylinder, rather than turn to fumes in the air when it's returned to the flame. Reheat and reshape as necessary to return to the blunt cylinder you started with.

Using the intense black stringer, apply six to eight stripes the length of the cylinder (photo 9). To do that, heat both the tip of the stringer and the spot where you intend to attach it, and touch the stringer to the cylinder, so that it's really stuck on. Then, holding the cylinder under the flame, use the radiant heat from the underside of the flame to let you press the stringer down the length of the cylinder, and then wrap it onto the face of the blunt end. Take a moment after each stringer is applied to heat it again and ensure that it's anchored well. (Leave a blunt end on the stringer—helpful if you decide to use it to create the pupil in the eye later.)

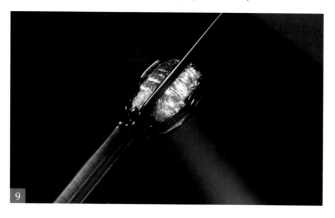

Attach a punty to the unattached end of the cylinder (I use a steel chopstick) (photo 10). Add a second chopstick punty in place of the glass rod (photo 11). Then warm the entire cylinder as you rock it first toward you and then away from you, to avoid adding a twist or allowing it to slump.

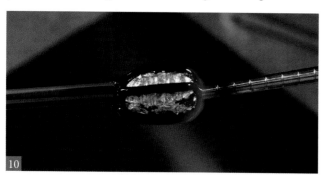

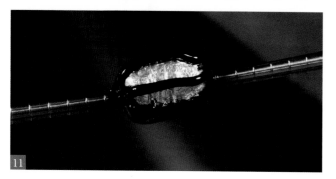

When the entire cylinder is molten to the core, hold it above the flame (still rocking it to keep it from slumping), and then slowly pull the cane until it's about 5 mm in diameter (photo 12). This cane is usually a little uneven, because the silver and frit heat and cool at different rates, which affects the diameter. That is a good thing, because the slices will vary slightly and cause every iris to be unique.

Allow the cane to cool, nip it free from the punties, and then cut it into murrini slices no more than ⅛ inch (3 mm) thick (photos 13 and 14). Even though the bead needs only two murrini—one for the eye on each side—I like to have a few extra in case I drop them as I work. Place the murrini on the edge of your torch-mounted marver (if you have one) to keep them warm.

workshop*wisdom*

Glass wants to be round, and yet glass that's applied to bead release is stuck there until it has cooled. If you make a tube and overheat it, the glass that isn't stuck to the bead release struggles to get round, pulling away from the holes toward the center of the bead. The resulting bead has the silhouette of a snake that swallowed a mouse, and the ends of the bead will be pointy. If you must heat the holes of a tube bead while the ends are still hot and malleable (perhaps because of the surface decoration being applied), gently roll them on the marver to cool them and freeze them in place, to avoid pointy ends.

MAKING THE BASE BEAD

To make the base bead, wind on a black tube about 1 inch (2.5 cm) long. Start by winding on the ends first, essentially creating two spacer beads about 1 inch (2.5 cm) apart—this will keep the ends of the tube nicely shaped—and then fill in with glass between the two spacers (photo 15). Because the tube is wider than the flame, when you heat the glass that you add between the spacers, the ends of the tube won't heat to the point of becoming molten, and thus won't draw in to the center and become pointy.

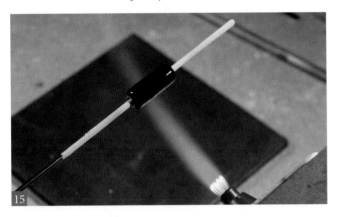

To make a barrel shape, add additional wraps of glass to the center four-fifths of the tube (photos 16 and 17). Melt the added glass smooth, and then add even a little more to the center one-fourth of the bead. This will result in a barrel shape (photo 18), which will flatten into a tab shape, which will have contours that mimic the shape of the eye.

APPLYING THE ENAMEL AND AVENTURINE

In Session 9, the Glass Portal bead, we'll sift enamel onto the outer surface of a bead, using a basket sifter (see page 110). Here, however, we roll the bead in a heatproof dish of enamel, applying a thicker layer. Some artists prefer this method because it creates less enamel dust in the air.

Simply bring the surface of the barrel bead to a uniform glow, then roll it in the enamel until no more will adhere (photo 19). Return the bead to the flame and heat the enamel until it's smooth. Don't rush. The enamel has a tendency to bubble and boil, but at this stage we want to make sure it's adhered, which is best achieved by slow, even heat. Keep adding enamel until the entire surface of the bead is white.

After the enamel is adhered to the bead, once again reheat the surface to a glow (photo 20), and roll the bead in the aventurine frit (photo 21). Reheat and re-apply where nothing stuck. I like the irregularities that the aventurine naturally creates, so I don't work at an even surface. I just let the aventurine go wherever it wants.

Heat the bead so that you can see the white enamel bubbling and boiling on the surface. This boiling disrupts the aventurine and causes the enamel to react with the copper, resulting in an array of color effects from brown to blue-green to verdigris. A little of the aventurine sparkle also usually remains. It's tricky to superheat this bead, boiling the surface, without also losing the barrel shape. If the bead becomes too soupy, allow it to cool, and then once again heat the surface. If the core of the bead has cooled down, then the surface can be heated with less risk of distorting the shape.

SHAPING THE EYE

When you are happy with the enamel-aventurine effect, it's time to *tabulate*, or flatten, the bead. Warm the length of the entire bead, from one hole to the other, and continue rotating it right up to the moment that you press it with the mashers (photo 22). If you stop too long to position the bead, odds are you won't get a symmetrical tabular shape.

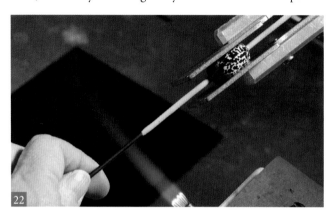

On each side of the bead, place a large dot of the light teal glass in the center (photo 23) and, using a handheld marver, flatten the dot until it's almost flush with the surface. Remembering to rewarm the bead after each step, apply a large dot of transparent black on top of the flat teal dot, and flatten the black (photos 24 and 25). Very little of the teal should

be visible around the black. It's there to create a shadow and give the black a little visual depth.

Apply a white dot in the center of each black dot, and press it flat. There should be some black visible around the perimeter of the white dot (photos 26 and 27). Alternate pressing and heating the stack of three dots until they're virtually flush with the surface of the bead.

Give the bead an overall reheating before the next step, and reheat it again each time you rake, to avoid cracking the bead. After reheating, hold the black rod with the attached fat stringer in your dominant hand, and direct the heat of the flame at the right side of the stack of dots, at the 3 o'clock position. You'll know that the right spot is molten—and thus ready to be worked—when the white glass becomes virtually transparent.

Raise the bead just above the flame and touch the black stringer to the black dot, just outside the white dot. Pull the black glass dot to the right until it will no longer move. Keep in mind that you're not digging into the bead with the stringer, just wiping the glass across the surface. The black glass you're trying to stretch is a wafer-thin layer on top of the base bead (photo 28). As you pull the black glass to your right, the black will stretch, and so will the white. The eye will taper, and the thinned black will have a purple hue. Repeat this process on the left (or 9 o'clock) side (photo 29).

APPLYING THE MURRINI

After you like the shape of the eye on each side of the bead, it's time to apply the murrini, which will serve as the iris. Pick up a murrini slice with pointy tweezers and wave it in the back of the flame to gently introduce it to the heat (photo 30). The murrini can be shocky—it's made of two glasses and silver, and it hasn't been annealed—so handle it gingerly. (If you have a waiting kiln available and can prewarm the murrini, it eliminates the shock factor almost entirely.)

workshop*wisdom*

Sometimes students have trouble heating the stack of dots without distorting the tabular shape of the bead, which usually means they aren't directing the flame at the right spot. The flame of the torch directs heat like an arrow from your abdomen out into the room. The dots on the bead should be at right angles to that arrow, so that the heat is pointed directly at the white dot. Avoid pointing the white dot toward the ceiling while the bead is in the flame, which causes the arrow of heat to aim at the edge of the bead, distorting its shape.

After the murrini is warm, direct the heat at the center of the eye, and wait for the white to become almost clear. Then, just outside the flame, place the murrini on the eye with the tweezers, and quickly press the murrini down into the white glass as far as possible, using a marver or other tool (photo 31).

Reheat the murrini and poke the fat black stringer or intense black stringer into its center; this will be the pupil, and the poke will draw the stripes of the iris into the center of the eye (photo 32). Blow on the spot where the stringer enters the glass, and move it sharply to the right or left; it will snap off. Gently rewarm the spot where the stringer detached so that no sharp edge is left behind.

EMBELLISHING THE EDGES

The edges of this bead are decorated with a stripe of the teal glass. Create a gather on the end of the teal rod, and then warm the edge of the bead where you intend to apply the stripe. Slightly reheat the gather, touch down at one end of the edge, and drag the glass the length of the bead (photo 33), using heat to disconnect the gather. Warm the stripe thoroughly onto the surface of the bead. Using a tool such as kitchen knife or dental spatula, carve grooves the length of the teal stripe (photo 34). This also helps ensure the glass is well attached. Add a similar stripe to the opposite edge of the bead (photos 35 and 36).

workshop*wisdom*

Sometimes when I make this bead, the white glass around the pupil has a yellowish tinge when the finished bead has cooled. This is from the metals in the murrini cane used for the pupil. Although I haven't found a way to eliminate it when using the cane described here, you can avoid that effect by using many other combinations of glass in the cane.

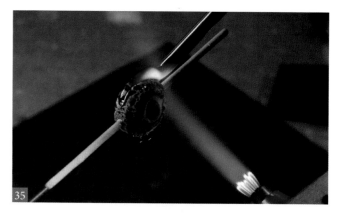

An undecorated background gives a more traditional appearance to the eye. The bead at the top shows a traditional pupil instead of a murrini.

1

2

3

Project Testers

Almost every member of the group attempted this bead and submitted several examples of finished beads and their "near misses." It's generous of them to so openly share their mistakes, in hopes of helping others find their way. Hayley described her first bead **(PHOTO 1)** as "disastrous," because she was unhappy with the thick eyelashes, applied with a full rod. Nonetheless, her use of silver laden glass produced a beautiful background and an interesting effect in the murrini she created. Her successful version of this bead has the lashes she was striving for and a more distinct murrini **(PHOTO 2)**.

The Project Testers had mixed results with the use of the aventurine frit and enamel for the background of the bead. Not everyone was pleased with the muted colors, although Jackie gave us an example of using that combination with reduced dots that worked perfectly with the color palette **(PHOTO 5)**. Several artists used copper leaf with enamel, boiling the surface enamel to produce a verdigris green. This, too, was very successful, as demonstrated by Debby's eye **(PHOTO 8)** and Sharon's large cabochon **(PHOTO 9)**. Hannah and Ginny included the aventurine, but Hannah combined it with silver, over a transparent glass base **(PHOTO 4)**. Ginny's bead, which re-orients the eye at right angles to the hole, has a beautiful background achieved using aventurine frit so fine that Ginny describes it as "almost powder" **(PHOTO 3)**.

Other examples of visually powerful backgrounds can be seen in the beads by Carolyn

4

5

6

7

8

9

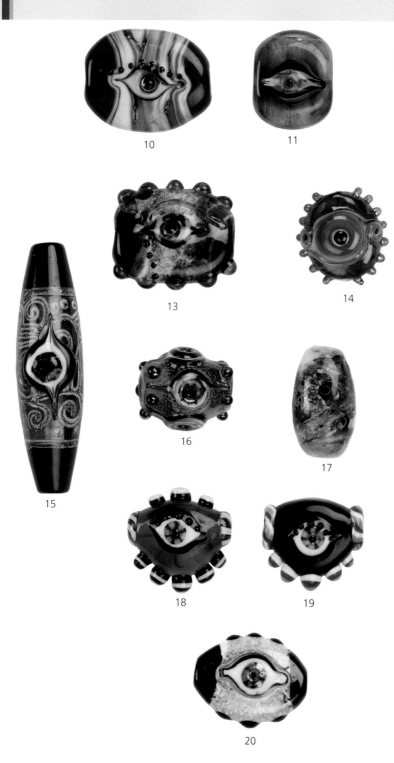

10

11

12

13

14

15

16

17

18

19

20

(PHOTO 10), Wendy (PHOTO 11), Emma (PHOTO 14), and Ann (PHOTO 12), all of whom moved away from enameled backgrounds in favor of color combinations that were more distinct.

Although the original project bead was a single eye, akin to the mystical eyes of many cultures, some artists incorporated the eye into a face or talisman. Hannah describes hers (PHOTO 34) as "an eye tooth claw thing" inspired by fellow artist Pipyr. Debby included the eye in two abstract faces (PHOTOS 33 AND 35), and Carolyn's cane provided eyes for the lizard perched on her bead (PHOTO 32).

Most group members created their eyes in muted colors, similar to the original project. Jen executed two of her eyes as pendants—the hole runs through the top third of the bead—and used what she felt were fun and approachable colors to avoid the evil eye connotation (PHOTOS 18 AND 19).

It can be difficult to move the eye bead onto a different shaped base, but Ali, Hannah, and Carolyn all succeeded. Ali's bicone is covered in silvered ivory stringer scrollwork, on which the eye seems to float (PHOTO 15). Carolyn buried the eye dots in a barrel that she then encased (PHOTO 17), and Hannah arrayed five eyes around the belly of a silvered ivory barrel (PHOTO 16).

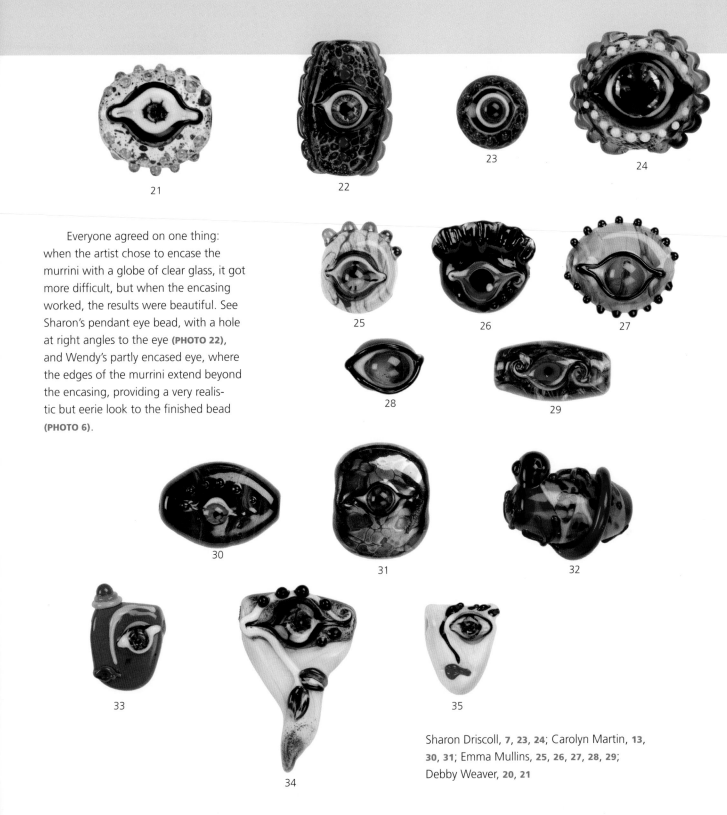

21

22

23

24

Everyone agreed on one thing: when the artist chose to encase the murrini with a globe of clear glass, it got more difficult, but when the encasing worked, the results were beautiful. See Sharon's pendant eye bead, with a hole at right angles to the eye **(PHOTO 22)**, and Wendy's partly encased eye, where the edges of the murrini extend beyond the encasing, providing a very realistic but eerie look to the finished bead **(PHOTO 6)**.

25

26

27

28

29

30

31

32

33

34

35

Sharon Driscoll, **7, 23, 24**; Carolyn Martin, **13, 30, 31**; Emma Mullins, **25, 26, 27, 28, 29**; Debby Weaver, **20, 21**

Claudia Trimbur-Pagel
Christmas, 2009
1¼ x ⅜ inches (3.1 x 1.1 cm)
Soft glass, murrini
Photo by artist

Marcy Lamberson
Untitled, 2010
1¼ x ¾ x ¼ inches (3.2 x 2 x .8 cm)
Soft glass; flameworked
Photo by artist

Margo Knight
Night and Day, 2010
Left to right, 1¼ x 1 x ¹¹⁄₁₆ inches (3.1 x 2.5 x 1.7 cm);
        1⅛ x 1 x ¹¹⁄₁₆ inches (2.9 x 2.5 x 1.7 cm)
Soft glass; flame worked, masked, etched
Photo by artist

Jeannie H. Cox
Dragon Eyes, 2010
2¼ x 1⅛ x ⅝ inches (5.7 x 3 x 1.5 cm)
Soft glass; flameworked
Photo by artist

Patricia Sage
Eye Bead, 2010
1⅜ x 1¼ x ⅝ inches (3.5 x 3.1 x 1.7 cm)
Soft glass; flameworked
Photo by Becky Dahlstedt

Sharlyn Premuda
Murrini Pushpins, 2010
Each ¾ x ⅜ x ⅜ inches (1.8 x 1 x 1 cm)
Soft glass; flameworked
Photo by artist

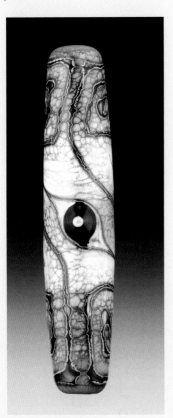

Margaret Zinser
Maze, 2008
1⅝ x 1⅛ inches (4 x 3 cm)
Soft glass, vitreous enamel, oxidized
    aventurine; flameworked
Photo by artist

Holly Cooper
Maora, 2010
1¼ x ⅝ inches (3.3 x 1.5 cm)
Soft glass, aventurine powder, silver leaf
Photo by artist

Jinx Garza
Oculi Volantes (Flying Eyes), 2010
2⅛ x ½ inches (5.3 x 1.4 cm)
Soft glass; double helix
Photo by Jerry Anthony

Margo Knight
Raven's Eye, 2009
1⅛ x ⅝ x ½ inches (3 x 1.7 x 1.4 cm)
Soft glass; flameworked, masked,
    etched
Photo by artist

Cosmic Bead

The "galaxies" in this bead are captivating, perhaps because they're magnified by the deep, transparent encasement. The glow-in-the-dark funnels, or "vortices," on the surface mimic imaginary black holes in space.

What Will This Session Teach?

In making this bead, you'll apply silver leaf to create a heavy stripe of silver globules on the interior surface. You'll learn to manipulate the glass using a thick stringer, and to add glow frit for the impression of distant galaxies. This bead also affords a chance to practice deep clear encasing, which is a challenge for many beadmakers.

Glass & Materials
Glass rods Ⓐ
- Black
- Opaque light sky blue
- Transparent aqua
- Transparent medium amethyst
- Pastel dark rose
- Ink blue
- Clear

Silver foil (page 38) Ⓓ

Root-beer-colored transparent glass
  with green dichroic coating,
  ½ inch (1.3 cm)-wide strip, slumped Ⓒ

Glow glass frit, aqua Ⓑ

Tools
Basic hand tools (page 6)
Baz Box (page 16)

Notes on Tools and Materials

Dichroic-coated glass A dichroic coating is a colorless mixture of vapors extracted from certain oxides and deposited onto glass in a vacuum chamber. Essentially, that colorless barrier acts as a filter that affects the colors seen by our eyes.

Dichroic coatings are available in many colors and patterns. If you're new to the material, you might want to buy a package of scraps, available from many suppliers, so you can practice before investing in pricier products.

I have the best success with dichroic-coated glass that has been cut into strips and slightly slumped in a kiln. These slumped strips cost a bit more, but I use them more efficiently and with less waste. Little "dichro" scraps left over from other projects also work.

Always make sure that the COE of your dichroic-coated glass is compatible with the other glass you're using, because the dichroic coating is available on many different types of glass.

Glow glass frit This frit is made of a specialty glass that glows in the dark after it's charged by exposure to light. According to the manufacturer, one minute of light exposure will result in a short-term glow, but an hour of strong sunlight will result in hours of glow. When heated in the bead, this frit fractures into a powdery appearance that reminds me of the Milky Way. Although it isn't essential, if you have a torch-mounted marver, keep three or four large chunks of frit on it, to warm for later use.

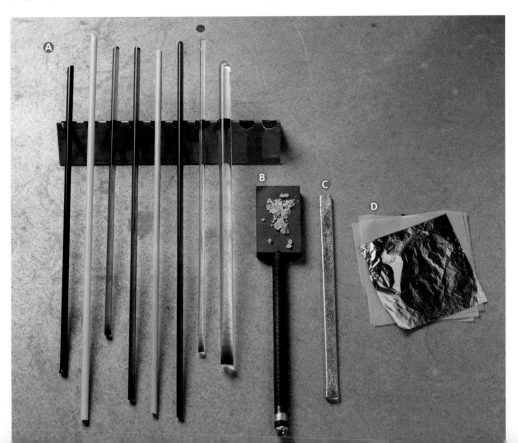

An Overview

This version of a galaxy bead is impressive in the round, as shown here, or in a lentil or tabulated shape. The deep encasing creates a "paperweight" effect that magnifies the swirling colors, flashes of dichro, and silver globes.

Creating the Bead

TWISTING THE FOIL

Before lighting the torch, you'll need to prepare the silver foil. Cut or tear off about one-third of a leaf, and twist it into a rope, as if you were twisting the paper wrapper from a drinking straw (photo 1). When you apply this silver rope to the bead, it will turn into little globules of silver.

PULLING THE STRINGER

You'll need to pull a short, fat stringer at the end of a 4 to 5 mm rod of clear glass, leaving it attached to the rod. This stringer will be your tool for creating the vortices in the surface of the bead.

With one hand, heat a small gather at the end of a clear rod. When the gather is glowing, come out of the flame and pinch the tip of the gather with serrated tweezers. Pull the stringer  when the glow has entirely subsided and the glass has gotten stiff, to make a thick stringer (about 3 mm) (photo 2). Use a nipper to leave a blunt end on the fat stringer.

> ### workshop*wisdom*
> Another great effect is to melt small balls of fine silver wire onto the surface. Make sure you're using *fine* silver, because sterling will turn black and unattractive. Thin wire of about 22 or 24 gauge works best. Be careful to hold the wire at a spot distant from where the wire meets the flame (or with tweezers), because it can transmit heat easily.

ENCASING THE DICHROIC COATING

Dichroic coating is susceptible to burning away in the heat of the torch. When using dichroic-coated *clear* glass, the usual secret is to place the strip of glass on a bead with the coating facing down, against the bead, and direct the heat of the torch at the glass. We don't have that luxury here. If the dichroic coating were sandwiched between the root beer glass and the black base bead, the dichro would be almost totally obscured—which defeats our purpose! Although it's possible to just melt the dichroic strip as gingerly as possible and have the coating survive the direct heat of the flame, an encasing step almost always guarantees greater success and brighter dichro.

Hold the dichroic-coated strip in your nondominant hand, as though it were a rod of glass, and introduce it to the cooler part of the flame, directing the heat primarily at the uncoated glass (photo 3). Gently warm about 1½ to 2 inches (3.8 to 5.1 cm) of the end of the strip, but don't get it so hot that it begins to deform or glow.

In your other hand, gather the end of a rod of clear glass. Starting at one edge of the strip, coat the dichroic side of the strip with clear glass by painting the gathers onto it (photo 4). To avoid creating air bubbles between the swipes of glass, place each swipe slightly on the edge of the preceding one. After the dichroic side is covered edge to edge, you have encased the dichroic coating, because on one side it is protected by the root beer transparent glass, and on the other side by clear encasing.

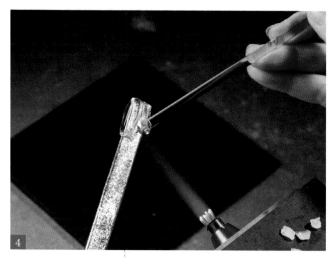

Heat it and press it flat with a marver, so that it's still "strip shaped" but thicker than the unencased strip (photo 5). Using the clear rod as a punty at the end of the strip, warm the encased portion, and then pull it into a strip that's about half the original width. It might be a little wonky, because this takes practice, but that won't matter (photo 6).

enough, and keep the tube as skinny as you can (photos 9, 10, and 11). (For a few hints on making a tube bead, see page 17.)

workshop*wisdom*

If you have only a short piece of dichroic-coated glass, start the encasing process by attaching it to a spare rod of glass, and use that as the handle to hold the strip while you encase it (photos 7 and 8).

Generally, I encase the strip just before I use it, so it's still warm from the encasing and not too shocky. If you encase the strip well in advance of making the bead, you might want to anneal the glass in your kiln, which will make it far less shocky when you reheat it.

Holding the glass at about a 45° angle to the base bead, coil the encased dichroic-coated strip around the bead, remembering to keep the root beer side of the strip against the black bead, so that the dichroic color faces out (photo 12). Heat the dichroic strip so it's well affixed to the bead, but don't melt it smooth (photo 13).

MAKING AND DECORATING THE BASE BEAD

The base bead is a skinny tube of black glass about ¾ inch (1.9 cm) long. If working with large amounts of glass is a challenge for you, make the tube ½ inch (1.3 cm) long and scale down the entire project. For some reason, even though I always remind students that this bead has a tendency to grow very large, they always start with an overly large initial footprint. It bears repeating: ¾ inch (1.9 cm) is plenty long

Next, heat the surface of the base bead so that it's just short of glowing hot. Remove it from the flame and wrap the twisted strip of silver foil onto it (photo 14), using tweezers to manipulate the foil into the grooves between the wraps of dichro. Before returning the bead to the flame, burnish the piece of silver with the outside of the tweezers so that the silver is in contact with the glass (photo 15). There's no need to reheat the bead at this point; both the silver and the bead will get enough heat in the next steps.

Using the pastel dark rose glass, apply three dots of glass asymmetrically around the bead (photo 16). Flatten each dot with a marver. Make a second dot of light sky blue on top of the pastel dark rose, and leave this second dot standing tall (photo 17). Then dot half of each "mountain" with the

transparent aqua (photo 18), and the other half with the transparent amethyst (photo 19). The only visible blue or pink should be at the base of the dot. (I have seen this called "half-dotting," but I tend to visualize it as each transparent glass encasing up one side of the mountain.) Apply a small dot of the ink blue glass at the base of the mountains, to finish covering up any bit of the opaque that is still exposed (photo 20). A little bit of ink blue goes a long way.

Add several pieces of glow glass frit to the bead, wherever you want them. I usually put a piece near the base of each covered dot, but not right up against it (photo 21). If you don't have any good chunks in your frit jar, just add more smaller pieces. It won't matter.

At this point, if you've followed my instructions to the letter, the bead is a lumpy and unsightly mess (photo 22), and it's hard to believe it will ever look like anything worth keeping. Don't give up!

Slowly begin to heat and rotate the bead. Your goal is to melt and smooth the surface so that although it remains irregular in shape, it becomes closer to round (photo 23). When you're done, the bead should have a softer contour—still irregular, but closer to symmetrical than when you started. In this heating, the silver leaf will melt and gather up into little balls of silver, and the dots will become big, soft bumps.

CREATING THE VORTICES

Allow the bead to cool a bit until any visible glow disappears. As you make the vortices, you'll be concentrating heat in specific spots and moving the heated glass. Although the bead should remain warm, you don't want it so hot that you distort the entire bead in the process.

Heat one of the dots and also a spot next to it; that spot is where you'll place the vortex (photo 24). When both are glowing hot, remove the bead from the flame and swipe the tip of the fat, clear stringer (still attached to its rod) over the mounded surface of the dot, dragging the colors into the vortex spot. Then plunge the stringer into the spot and rotate the rod in

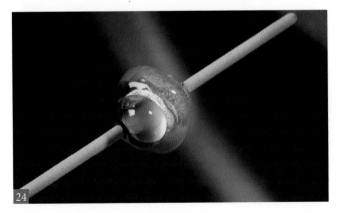

your fingers (in one direction only), so that the edge of the dot and the adjoining glow glass or dichroic glass are pulled into a twisting funnel (photos 25, 26, and 27).

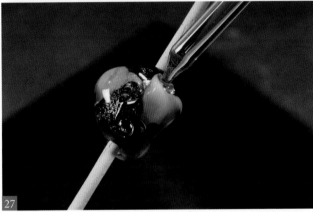

When you like the look of the twist (or when the glass won't move anymore), blow *hard* on the stringer where it touches the bead, and snap off the stringer by sharply moving the rod from side to side. Before you admire your work, rewarm the entire bead, because it has been out of the flame. If you've done this successfully, you've created a hole in the bead that looks like a whirlpool. You'll notice that the glow glass has a diffuse appearance, and that you have captured bits of silver and dichro in the swirls of glass.

workshop*wisdom*

Artist Lani Ching covers the entire surface of beads with these twists, which she refers to as "tessellations." This doesn't refer to the twisting pattern but to the fact that a tessellation is a collection of figures that cover a surface with no overlaps and no gaps.

Repeat this process, creating as many vortices as you want. After some practice, you can vary the size of the twists, the color of the stringer, or where on the bead you twist. Keep in mind that ultimately this bead will be encased and round, so don't create a grossly asymmetrical shape, or it will be very difficult to finish the bead. Instead, scatter the twists all over the surface with an eye toward rough symmetry. After I've made three deep whirlpools, I usually make many shallow twists.

Peaks and valleys, or irregular spots on the surface of the bead, will trap air bubbles when the bead is encased. I like that in this bead, because it seems more "spacey" to me. Before you begin encasing, take a moment to assess the shape of the bead; melt smooth any huge irregularities, and shape the bead closer to round. I like to leave the deep vortices in the surface, because I enjoy the added dimension they give the finished bead.

SWIPE ENCASING THE BEAD

This bead will be encased using a version of *swipe encasing*. The transparent glass is applied to the base bead by pressing gathers of molten glass onto the surface of the bead with a swiping motion. Each swipe ideally wraps all the way around the bead and slightly overlaps the one before.

workshop*wisdom*

Encasing is faster if you have large-diameter clear rods (approximately 10 mm). If you do, preheat their ends in your kiln, to avoid shocky glass and to shorten the time it takes to heat the rods at the torch (photo 28).

Start with a large, soupy gather of clear glass, and coil it onto the bead, beginning at one edge (photo 29). The important thing is to slightly overlap the coils so that you don't trap air bubbles (there will be plenty of bubbles in this bead anyway). This is your chance to make the bead symmetrical, so add extra clear where the bead seems out of round. Try to press the molten glass down into the vortices, to minimize bubbles. On each end, add an extra wrap of glass that extends beyond the base bead (photo 30). This "turtleneck" of glass will fall down the side of the bead, rounding it and encasing the side.

Now to melt the bead smooth. Start by focusing heat at the center third of the encasing, rotating the bead to keep it on center (photo 31). When this section is smooth and round, direct the heat to one end, still holding the bead at right angles to the flame. When half the encasing is smooth, angle the bead so that the flame is directed at the mandrel and into

the hole, which will cause the wrap of clear that is off the edge of the bead to fall down and encase the side (photo 32). Then return to the center of the bead, heat the clear to the second end, and encase the side in the same way (photo 33).

Examine the bead carefully from all angles, checking for symmetry, adding clear glass as needed. Your eyes are your most important tool in achieving a round bead.

As you heat and reshape this bead, its core will begin to grow hot. If you see more than a slight glow in the core bead, back off the heat until the glow subsides. You want to move and shape the clear encasing, but you don't want the core bead to move and flow; that would distort the surface design.

As I completed this bead, I noticed a small piece of dirt or soot in the clear encasing. To remove it, I heated only the dirty area, and plucked the clear glass from the bead with a pointed tweezers (photo 34), being careful to remove as little glass as possible and to avoid heating the bead to its core, which would have made it susceptible to distortion from the plucking.

When you're happy with the shape (and, by the way, this bead can also be pressed into a great pendant), give the bead one more overall heating, so that it's uniformly warm throughout. When it's not glowing at all, put it in the kiln to anneal (photo 35).

workshop*wisdom*

Although I like bubbles in this bead, too many large ones ruin the overall effect, so after the bead is encased, I sometimes remove a bubble or two. If you want to do likewise, allow the bead to cool, then direct the intense heat of the flame at the bubble. With luck, it will rise close to the surface. (Sometimes you have to cool and reheat the bubble a few times before it will cooperate.) If it pops through the surface, well and good. If not, some artists use pointy tweezers to reach into the encasing and grab the bubble. I prefer to touch a clear rod to the heated surface of the encasing and pull up long threads of clear glass. The bubble eventually rises up into the thread and can be discarded. Finally, reheat the surface and, if necessary, add a small amount of clear to replace what you've removed.

Extra glow frit lends a fuzzy interior to the cosmic swirls.

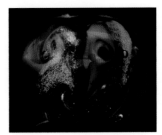

The glow-in-the-dark feature is a playful addition to the cosmic bead.

1

2

3

4

5

6

7

8

9

10

11

12

13

14

15

16

Project Testers

The group tackled this bead with gusto, with ten members submitting examples of their work. Several commented that they had long intended to attempt this style of bead and were pleased with the results. As Sharon commented, "These beads were just plain fun to do!"

One challenge is the bead's tendency to grow quite large. Hayley **(PHOTO 1)**, Ali **(PHOTO 4)**, and Ann **(PHOTO 2)** embraced this characteristic, used it to their advantage, and rendered wonderful pendants that were deeply encased and an impressive 2½ inches (6.4 cm) long. Ann also did a plump round bead, 2½ inches (6.4 cm) in diameter **(PHOTO 3)**.

An occasional cracked bead seemed to be caused by the glow frit, but a heavier encasing layer solved the problem. Group members who used many different brands of glass, and silver glass, also occasionally encountered some cracks. Emma had some cracking problems that she ultimately attributed to "messing around with the beads for too long and not warming them properly before putting them in the kiln." The cracked beads she provided **(PHOTOS 5 AND 6)** display a straight crack that runs from hole to hole on the bead, which is typical of a thermal fracture, meaning a crack that results from the bead getting too cold.

Jen's insertion of copper stars and small pieces of aventurine frit **(PHOTOS 8 AND 23)** and Sharon's addition of teeny cubic zirconia **(PHOTO 24)** are well displayed in these large, tabular beads. Jen noted that she decorated only one side of the tab, because "it was hard enough to manage positioning the various bits and pieces and to get everything encased." Jen calls her bead *Cosmic Party* because her blue dichro is "vibrant"— an effect she enhanced with dabs of transparent cobalt.

This bead lends itself to variations in shape, which the group ably explored. Sharon created a cosmic cabochon for her pendant and a teardrop cosmos **(PHOTOS 31 AND 32)**. Hannah

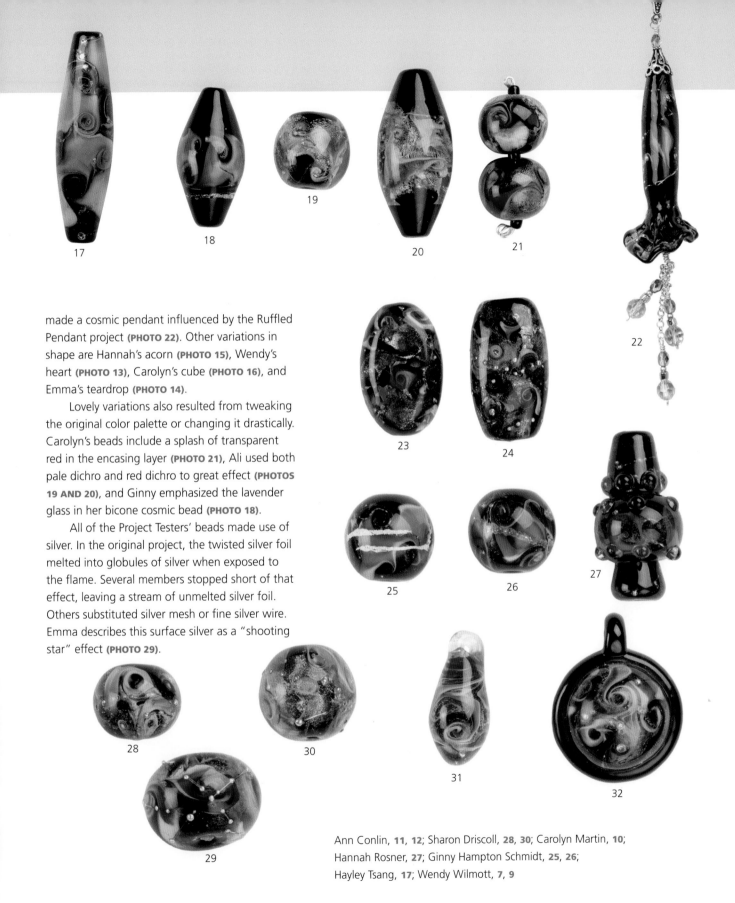

made a cosmic pendant influenced by the Ruffled Pendant project **(PHOTO 22)**. Other variations in shape are Hannah's acorn **(PHOTO 15)**, Wendy's heart **(PHOTO 13)**, Carolyn's cube **(PHOTO 16)**, and Emma's teardrop **(PHOTO 14)**.

Lovely variations also resulted from tweaking the original color palette or changing it drastically. Carolyn's beads include a splash of transparent red in the encasing layer **(PHOTO 21)**, Ali used both pale dichro and red dichro to great effect **(PHOTOS 19 AND 20)**, and Ginny emphasized the lavender glass in her bicone cosmic bead **(PHOTO 18)**.

All of the Project Testers' beads made use of silver. In the original project, the twisted silver foil melted into globules of silver when exposed to the flame. Several members stopped short of that effect, leaving a stream of unmelted silver foil. Others substituted silver mesh or fine silver wire. Emma describes this surface silver as a "shooting star" effect **(PHOTO 29)**.

Ann Conlin, **11**, **12**; Sharon Driscoll, **28**, **30**; Carolyn Martin, **10**; Hannah Rosner, **27**; Ginny Hampton Schmidt, **25**, **26**; Hayley Tsang, **17**; Wendy Wilmott, **7**, **9**

Larry Scott
Night Sky Bead, 2010
1⅞ x ⅞ x ⅞ inches (4.5 x 2.1 x 2.1 cm)
Soft glass, fine silver foil, wire
Photo by artist

Andrea Guarino-Slemmons
Capped Galaxy, 2010
¾ inch (1.8 cm) in diameter
Soft glass; silver fumed
Photo by artist

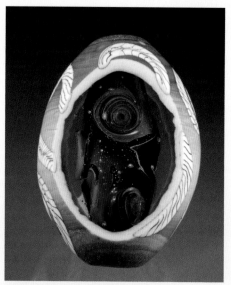

Andrea Guarino-Slemmons
Galaxy Within, 2009
1¾ x 1¼ x ¾ inches (4.4 x 3.1 x 2 cm)
Soft glass; silver fumed, flat lapped
Photo by artist

Carol White
Cosmic Cones, 2007
Left to right, 1⅛ x ¾ x ¾ inches (3 x 2 x 2 cm);
    1⅝ x ¾ x ¾ inches (4 x 2 x 2 cm);
    1⅜ x ¾ x ¾ inches (3.5 x 2 x 2 cm)
Soft glass, silver foil; flameworked
Photo by Larry Johnson, Jr.

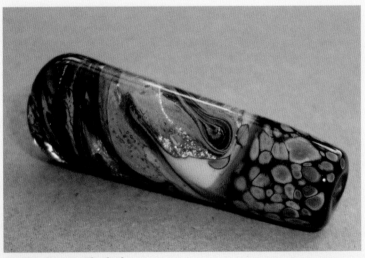

Cynthia Burton Cheslock
Silver Blue Swirl, 2009
1¾ x ⅛ inches (4.5 x 0.3 cm)
Soft glass; flameworked
Photo by artist

D. Lynne Bowland
Parting Company, 2010
1⅞ x ⅞ x ¾ inches (4.5 x 2.1 x 2 cm)
Soft glass, enamels, cane, goldstone; flameworked,
    ground, cold polished
Photo by artist

Mirrored Rainbow Hollow

This bead is a showstopper. Light and airy, it's great for many kinds of jewelry. When the interior is mirrored, the bead seems to glow with a mysterious inner light.

What Will This Session Teach?

This bead reinforces the skills needed to make a hollow bead, using either a traditional mandrel or a Puffy Mandrel, and enhances those skills by requiring that you apply each color of the rainbow in roughly equal amounts. Later, you'll also learn to add a mirror finish inside the bead.

Glass & Materials

Glass rods  (A)
- Transparent lapis
- Transparent medium aqua
- Transparent yellow
- Transparent orange
- Transparent red
- Transparent light blue
- Transparent emerald green

Tools

- Basic hand tools (page 6)
- Puffy Mandrel, ⅛ inch (3 mm) in diameter (D)
- Stamp tweezers (C)
- Raw polymer clay, small scrap (B)
- Mirroring supplies (see Appendix A, page 131)

Notes on Tools and Materials

Puffy Mandrel So named because you puff air into it, a Puffy Mandrel is a hollow tube with a small hole drilled into its side about 2 inches (5.1 cm) from one end. To prep it, dip about one-third of the mandrel in bead release—the third that includes the side hole—and blow into the other end with a short, sharp puff of air. The side hole should clear, leaving the far end of the mandrel still plugged. If the end also clears, redip the tip to seal it.

For this project we'll use a Puffy Mandrel of larger than usual diameter, resulting in larger bead holes. Big bead holes are helpful with multistrand projects, because several strands of beading wire can fit through the holes, but they're especially useful if you intend to fill and empty the bead with the solutions that create an interior mirror. That's just easier with a large hole.

An Overview

A hollow bead is made from two disks of glass sealed around a small pocket of air. In this bead we'll create the disks from a rainbow-themed assortment of glass, seal the disks, and then inflate the bead with a puff of breath.

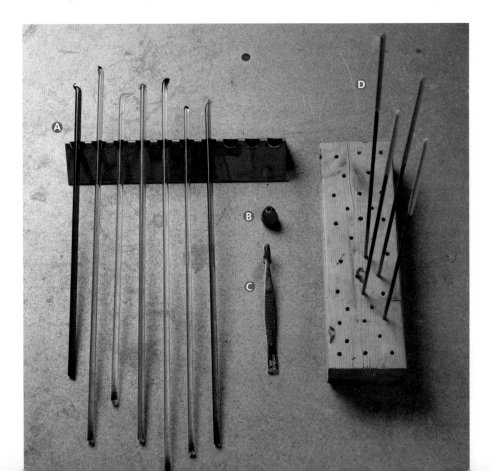

The mirrored interior of this sandblasted bead gives the illusion of great depth.

Creating the Bead

At the outset, give some thought to your choice of glass. Even if all your glass has the same COE, it can vary in viscosity (or fluidity) when molten. For my bead, I stayed with various colors of transparent Italian glass. In my experience, the colors will expand and contract at pretty much the same rate. This means that when the hot bead is inflated, all the stripes will expand equally, keeping the surface smooth.

FORMING THE FIRST TWO DISKS

The footprint of this bead (its ultimate width) is established by two spacer-size disks of glass, one of transparent lapis and one of transparent red, each about two wraps of glass tall. It's important to keep your wraps consistent in size, so that you have enough room for all the colors of the rainbow. This can be tough, because you're building the bead from the holes inward and meeting in the middle.

These first two disks are all that anchor a hollow bead to the mandrel, so it's important that they be well adhered to the bead release. If they aren't, the weight of additional wraps of glass can cause them to break free and rotate freely, and excess air can escape at the bead holes when you blow to inflate the bead. Be sure to preheat the bead release to a glow and apply molten wraps of glass. If the glass doesn't stick to the bead release as it touches it, the bead release probably isn't hot enough.

To make the lapis disk, create a gather on the end of the lapis rod. Rotate the rod as you hold the tip in the flame, or rock it toward you and then away from you, so that the gather is round and drawn equally from the entire circumference of the glass rod (photo 1).

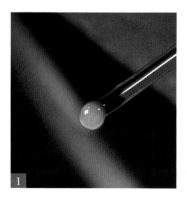

workshop*wisdom*

If you're struggling with the concept that different glass has different viscosity, experiment. Try making a hollow bead out of a combination of Italian and German transparent glasses—or opaque and transparent glass from a single manufacturer—and watch what happens. When these mixed-glass beads are inflated, the surface of the bead will be slightly rippled or ridged, because the different colors expand differently. (Of course, this can be a very cool effect if it's planned.)

workshop*wisdom*

Students often complain that they run out of molten gather before they've applied an entire wrap of glass. (When they run short, they tend to stretch out the last little bit of glass to finish the wrap, ending up with disks that are uneven in thickness.) This is usually because they've gathered one side of the rod but left the other side cooler and unmelted. The cooler glass causes the gather to stiffen more quickly, and leaves less molten glass to work with.

Position the mandrel just behind the flame, and hold the gather at right angles to the mandrel, passing through the flame. Begin rolling the mandrel away from you. Touch the gather to the rolling mandrel about ½ inch (1.3 cm) from the side hole, and roll the disk onto the mandrel (photo 2). Ideally, apply two revolutions of glass and then disconnect.

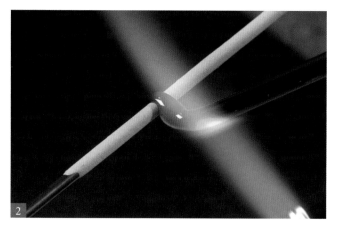

To leave a smooth tapered trail, continue to roll the mandrel away from you, and increase the distance between the mandrel and the rod of glass, moving the mandrel closer to the table and the rod closer to your nose. This will thin the attachment between the two, and the flame will cut through that attachment without dumping more glass onto the disk.

All this attention to disks will stand you in good stead as you build this bead. In other hollow bead designs, uneven disks (or small holes between the wraps of glass) won't show or can be repaired. For this bead, any repairs will likely distort the stripes of color. This isn't fatal, but it won't fully achieve the rainbow appearance you're after.

workshop*wisdom*

If your initial disks are symmetrical but too round, they can be tweaked if you have stamp tweezers (a.k.a. mini-mashers) on hand. Immediately after disconnecting the gather from the disk, while still rolling the mandrel, pass the disk through

the flame to keep it warm, and then hold it just above the flame. Quickly pinch the disk two or three times to diminish its width (photo 3). The tweezers should be at right angles to the mandrels and applied near, but not at, the mandrel. Make sure there's enough heat in the glass so that it will move with the tweezers, or you run the risk of breaking the bead release. Also remember to quench the tweezers frequently.

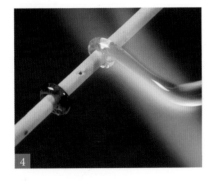

Now add a disk of transparent red about 1 to 1¼ inches (2.5 to 3.2 cm) away, on the opposite side of the hole (photo 4).

ADDING THE AQUA AND ORANGE

Next, apply the aqua glass on top of the lapis (photo 5) and then the orange on top of the red (photo 6). (Remember to keep both disks warm.) The goal is to create two taller disks that are approximately the same size.

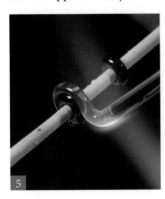

Both aqua and orange are added in a similar way. Create a gather on the end of the rod, but this time you'll need a larger gather, because the disks are larger. If you have trouble balancing the bigger gather, angle the cold end of the rod downward, so the gather is supported by the rod. Hold the mandrel so that the existing disk is just below the flame and the perimeter of the disk is almost glowing. Apply the gather at right angles, through the flame; the mandrel should be rotating away from you before the next wrap of glass is applied.

Remember to keep both disks warm by holding the mandrel at about a 45° angle to the flame, so the heat touches both disks. They shouldn't become molten, so if you see a glow in the glass, try a cooler spot in the flame (photo 7).

workshop*wisdom*

If either disk begins to spin freely on the mandrel and you don't think the bead release has cracked, perhaps the disk was never well adhered to the bead release. Before abandoning the bead, try heating the hole where the disk rests on the mandrel, in an effort to heat the bead release and the glass enough that they stick together. If the bead release under the disk is broken, try to build a bridge that will hold until you can finish the bead (photo 8).

ADDING THE YELLOW AND LIGHT BLUE

Instead of adding to the height of the disk, the next two colors—yellow and light blue—begin to curve the sides of the bead toward each other. Each side will form a C shape; the space between them will be filled with transparent green.

Of course, the gathers of yellow and light blue should be even larger than the previous ones, because the distance to be covered continues to grow.

To achieve the C shape, add the first wrap of light blue slightly inside the aqua wrap at the outer edge of the disk, and then continue the second wrap so that it curves even closer to the center (photo 9). Add the yellow glass in the same manner (photo 10). If you need to curve the disks using pressure from a marver, remember to heat only the color

you want to move, and roll the glass gently on the marver (photo 11). Too much pressure will break the disk from the bead release.

FILLING IN THE GREEN

If all has gone well, two wraps of green glass will complete the bead. Create a gather, touch one side of the gap in the bead, and add about two wraps (photo 12). If you've kept your disk warm as you worked, the bead will be far less shocky once the sides are connected. That's because you aren't keeping two separate disks warm, but rather one whole bead, with its own little pocket of warm air trapped inside.

INFLATING THE BEAD

As you warm the bead in preparation for inflating it, the molten glass will press down on the warm air inside, pushing it down through the blow hole and out the end of the mandrel, thus causing your bead to collapse. To prevent this, hold your finger or palm over the open end of the hollow tube, so the air can't escape. Another method was developed by beadmaker Barbara Becker Simon. She pushes a little piece of clay onto the open end of the tube and leaves it there until she's ready to inflate the bead (photo 13). Other bead-makers use tiny pieces of cork.

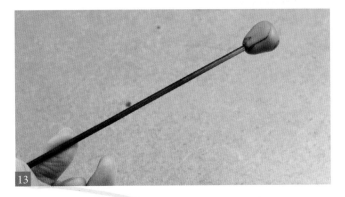

While blocking the open end of the tube, rotate the bead in the flame so that it gradually becomes molten (photo 14). Don't be surprised to see the bead shrink slightly as the surface gets molten; it won't collapse if the tube is closed off. Roll the bead in the flame, heating it gently and slowly so that it becomes round. Don't rush this step; you want to achieve an even heat base throughout the bead.

Rotating the bead so it stays on center, turn the mandrel around and gently press the open end against your mouth, to keep the air inside (photo 15). (Yes, remove the clay if

you were using it to seal the tube!) Continue to rotate, with the mandrel parallel to the table. Just as the glow of the glass subsides, blow one or two puffs of air into the bead. It takes practice to judge the right moment, but it's a lot like pulling stringer. The bead should be inflated just before it will be too stiff to expand. Keep rotating the bead until you're certain it will no longer droop.

Warm the bead in the back of the flame, and inspect it to make sure it's symmetrical. Although you can reheat and re-inflate the bead if you aren't happy, this usually distorts the stripes. With practice, you'll get it right. The bead is now ready to be annealed.

CLEANING THE BEAD

When the annealed bead is cool, soak the mandrel and bead in water and then use a damp paper towel to remove the bead release from around the bead. The bead should then easily twist off the mandrel. (Try not to use pliers to hold the mandrel, which will squeeze the mandrel and ruin it if you're unlucky.) Using a skinny mandrel or file, break up the excess bead release inside the bead, and then soak it in water overnight.

Hold the bead under running water to remove any remaining bead release, and then clean the holes. If there's stubborn bead release left behind (which is more common with smaller mandrels), try blowing it out the way you would blow out an egg; or use a dental irrigator or sink sprayer to force a stream of water into the bead. Tap out all excess water, and then dry the beads hole-side-up on a rack that allows air to circulate. That way, no moisture is trapped in the bead. When it's clean and dry, it's ready to be mirrored.

MIRRORING THE BEAD

To give the bead a mysterious, luminous glow, apply a silver mirrored finish to the interior of the bead. (See Appendix A on page 131 for information about mirroring.)

workshop*wisdom*

If your bead doesn't inflate symmetrically, it probably didn't have an even heat base; the hotter spots are ballooning out ahead of the cooler ones. Try to heat the bead slowly, with all-over heat, so that you're bringing the entire bead up to the same temperature. The other possible problem is the thickness of your glass. If some wraps are thicker than others, they won't inflate at the same rate. Although you can use stamp tweezers to thin your disks as you work, the true remedy is practice.

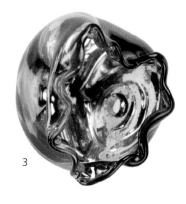

1

2

3

4

5

6

7

8

Project Testers

Everyone in the Project Testers group had experimented with hollow beads before. For some, the Puffy Mandrel was a new tool, one they enjoyed.

Both Emma **(PHOTO 2)** and Wendy **(PHOTO 1)** executed striped hollows in the style of the project bead, using a wide band of color for the center stripe (Emma's red, Wendy's blue) and narrower rings of color toward the holes. The widest color truly dominates the design.

Kristen **(PHOTO 14)** designed her beads in muted blues and greens in the 90 COE palette. Because the colors differ by only a few shades, the bead doesn't have obvious stripes. Instead, the colors seem to flow from one hole to the other in an interesting gradation.

Debby **(PHOTO 6)** and Jen **(PHOTO 7)** each tried a tone-on-tone pattern of color that didn't entirely measure up to their expectations. Debby's pale aqua bead was dabbed with a darker transparent blue, which she hoped would give a watery effect. Jen made a pale amethyst bead with darker purple dots around the holes. Both found that after mirroring, there wasn't enough contrast in the colors. In another attempt at this tone-on-tone effect, Debby made a transparent green bead and coated it in frit, which she

9

10

11

12

13

14

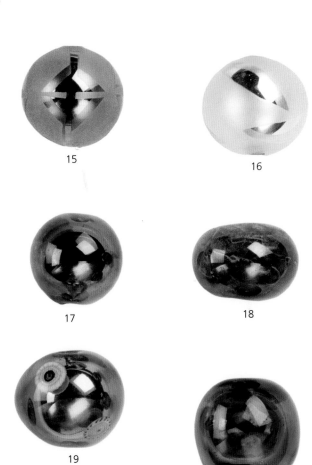

15

16

17

18

19

20

left in relief on the surface of the bead. The contrast in texture was very apparent after the bead was mirrored (**PHOTO 8**).

Sharon (**PHOTOS 11, 15, AND 16**) explored a tone-on-tone effect by sandblasting a mirrored bead, one of my favorite techniques. The pattern almost seems to float above the surface.

High-contrast surface decoration adds visual pop to a mirrored bead. Ann's (**PHOTOS 4 AND 5**) and Hannah's striped hollows (**PHOTOS 12 AND 13**), decorated with stringer, twisties, and dots, show the success of decoration that enhances but doesn't obscure the mirroring. Ann experimented with the look of silver laden glass for her bead decoration, because she was "intrigued by the concept of a layered silvered surface with colored transparents." Ann also found that the Puffy Mandrel enabled her to melt the outer design flush into the surface of the hollow, because she could re-inflate the bead as needed while heating in the design.

Wendy (**PHOTO 3**) submitted an exploded hollow with this little tale: "I was merrily beading when, of course, the doorbell rang. I popped my bead-in-progress into the kiln while I answered the door. Back at work, I returned my bead to the flame and gently reheated it. But it had slumped in the kiln and become thinner on one side, so when inflated, it *popped*! So I ruffled the edges and mirrored the inside, and I'll hang it on the Christmas tree next year!"

Krisitn Frantzen Orr, **17, 20**; Jen Place, **9**; Hannah Rosner, **18**; Debby Weaver, **19**; Sharon Driscoll, **10**

Bernadette Fuentés
Ancient Artifact, 2010
Height, 2¼ inches (5.7 cm)
Soft glass; blown, layered, cane work
Photo by Stewart O'Shields

Michael Mangiafico
Red Cancer, 2009
4¾ x 4¾ x 4¾ inches (12 x 12 x 12 cm)
Soft glass, hollow bead; flameworked
Photo by artist

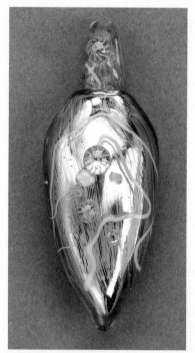

Patricia Sage
Lacey Bubbles, 2008
¾ x 1 x 1 inch (1.8 x 2.4 x 2.4 cm)
Soft glass; flameworked
Photo by Becky Dahlstedt

Bernadette Fuentés
Modern Artifact, 2010
Height, 2½ inches (6.4 cm)
Soft glass; blown, layered, cane work
Photo by Stewart O'Shields

Susan Hood
Phantasea Shell, 2009
1⅛ x 1⅛ x ¾ inches
(3 x 3 x 2 cm)
Soft glass; flameworked
Photo by Debbie Roberts

Laurie Salopek
Metamorphosis Focal Bead, 2006
2⅞ inches (7.3 cm)
Soft glass; flameworked
Photographer unknown

Ronnie Lambrou
Stardust, 2010
20½ inches (52.1 cm) long
Mirrored sandblasted beads by Jeri
    Warhaftig; crystals, Japanese
    seed beads
Photo by Panos Lambrou

Jari Ann Sheese
Untitled, 2010
Each, 3 x 2¾ inches (7.6 x 7 cm)
Soft glass; flameworked
Photo by Lori Naanes

Kim Fields
Meconopsis (Blue Poppies), 2009
⅞ x 1¼ x 1¼ inches (2.3 x 3.3 x 3.3 cm)
Soda-lime glass, enamel, crystals, copper
    findings, silver chain; lampworked,
    hollow worked
Photo by artist

Cane
Beads

Because these tubes are cold-worked
to the desired length, you can create
identical pairs for earrings or other
jewelry. When made entirely of
clear glass, they're completely
transparent, without the etched
hole left by a mandrel.

What Will This Session Teach?

In making this off-mandrel bead, you'll learn to manage an unusually large amount of glass, and to judge the heat base of that glass to pull a long, symmetrical cane.

Glass & Materials

Glass rods Ⓐ
> Opaque white
> Intense black stringer (page 37)
> Clear
> **Color Scheme 1**
>> A Transparent medium amber
>> B Transparent emerald green
> **Color Scheme 2**
>> A Transparent red
>> B Transparent yellow

Tools

Basic hand tools (page 6)

Two cabochon mandrels,
> ¾ inch (1.9 cm) in diameter Ⓑ

Graphite rod, ¼ to ½ inch
> (6 mm to 1.3 cm) in diameter Ⓒ

Wet saw or tungsten carbide scoring knife

Wet/dry sandpaper, 170 and 600 grit Ⓓ

Notes on Tools and Materials

Cabochon mandrels These were developed to assist bead-makers in making a cabochon-shaped piece of glass, without the through-piercing that makes a piece of glass a bead. The mandrel is essentially a coin-shaped piece of steel mounted at right angles to one end of a steel rod, so that the "coin" provides a platform for the glass. We'll use two of these mandrels as punties for this project. Try it first with the ¾-inch (1.9 cm) size, but if you're already comfortable with that size, challenge yourself to build the cylinder on a larger diameter mandrel. The task gets harder as the cylinder gets larger in diameter, because you need to keep all the glass hot enough to avoid cracking.

Graphite rod Graphite easily smooths molten glass without sticking to it. Available commercially in almost any diameter, graphite rods can be brittle if dropped, and because they tend to roll, the most convenient ones have a wooden handle that makes them less likely to tumble off the bench.

Glass cutter This project creates a tube of glass that will be sliced into individual beads. This can be done with a glass saw, although the saw blade nibbles away glass with each cut. I prefer a *tungsten carbide scoring knife*, sold specifically for cutting glass rods and tubing. Essentially, you score around the tube in one spot, dampen the score (saliva is traditional),

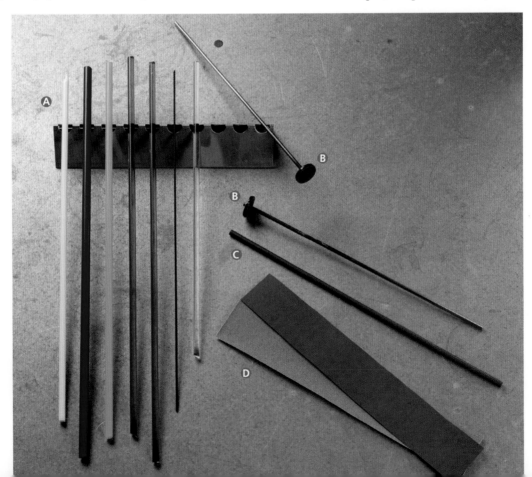

and snap the tube at the score line. Be sure to wear protective eyewear and snap the tube away from your body. Once you get the hang of this, you'll get a nice clean slice that doesn't use up any of the tube in the cutting process. It also works to use a glass cutter with a tungsten carbide wheel, such as the type sold for cutting sheet glass.

Sandpaper For the final finish of the tubes, we will use wet/dry sandpaper to sand the flat ends of the tubes. At a minimum, you'll want to use 170 grit (very coarse) and 600 grit (less coarse). You might also want to do a third sanding at 1200 grit to finish the beads—a matter of personal preference. If you have a flat lap grinder available, that will work also.

An Overview

Furnace-glass beads are made at a *glory hole* (a small furnace), where a large, hollow gather of glass is decorated and pulled into a long tube. These faux furnace glass beads are made at the torch, using a method based on instructions written some years ago by beadmaker Larry Scott, and updated with the use of the cabochon mandrels and the wet/dry sanding or grinding.

Creating the Bead

I've suggested two possible color schemes for these beads, but once you've made a few, you'll find that there are many possible color variations. I like the appearance of a solid white core, because the transparent colors appear more saturated against a white background.

> ### workshop*wisdom*
> When creating the glass surface on the first punty, be sure to wrap the clear glass around the rim of the steel so that it can't come off until it's shocked off. Otherwise, while it's holding in the kiln, it will cool down and can pop off the mandrel. Essentially, you want retention of the glass around the rim of the steel disk.

PREPARING THE CABOCHON MANDRELS

Preheat one of the cabochon mandrels in the flame until it's nearly glowing hot (photo 1). Using the clear glass, coat the rim and the face of the flat surface with about a 2-mm thickness of clear glass that extends slightly beyond, and around the edges of, the steel disk (photo 2). (Using the coin analogy, cover the rim of the coin and one entire side.) Use a marver to press the glass flat on the face of the disk (photo 3).

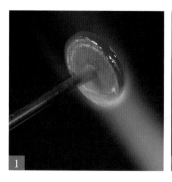

Put the glass-coated mandrel—its handle will act as a steel punty—in a waiting kiln. Make sure that enough of the mandrel is sticking out of the kiln to let you grab cool steel when you need this punty.

After one punty is safely in the kiln, coat the rim of the remaining mandrel with clear glass in the same manner. We're using clear glass for this because it's stiffer than the white glass, and will make it easier to keep the core cylinder from slumping in the final heating-and-pulling stage. Be careful to wrap the clear glass around the edges of the steel so that it's tightly adhered (photo 4).

MAKING THE CORE CYLINDER

The core of the cylinder is made of opaque white glass. It's built on the outer edge of the clear glass, so it's actually slightly larger than the ¾-inch (1.9 cm) steel disk that is the cabochon mandrel.

Start by winding on one ring of white glass, keeping in mind that it should be cylindrical (photo 5), and that the goal is to avoid decreasing the center of the cylinder. As you build the cylinder, the graphite rod comes in handy to smooth the interior of the cylinder and also to push out the walls of the cylinder in the event that they begin to collapse inward.

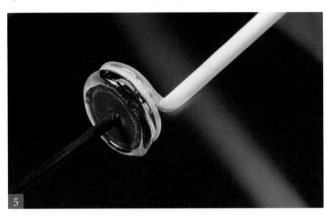

The goal is to coil on white glass until the cylinder is at least 1 inch (2.5 cm) tall and to create this shape with a smooth interior and exterior. Naturally, it's tricky to keep the cylinder from collapsing while still introducing enough heat to achieve a smooth surface. If you're struggling with this, try using the graphite rod to make the cylinder slightly wider in diameter, which will make it less prone to collapse (photos 6 and 7).

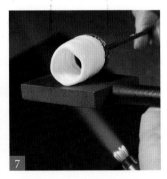

The next step is to add another layer of white so that the core cylinder is a double thickness of white glass. You could coil on the white in the same way you created the initial core, but I prefer to use what is called "swipe encasing" to add the next layer. (We did a bit of swipe encasing on the Cosmic Bead, page 56.) It will help smooth out any residual ring indentations from the initial coiling, and will also add a thicker layer of white than is typically added with a coil.

To start, create a large gather of glass on the end of the white rod. Then touch it down at the open end of the cylinder, and swipe the glass the length of the cylinder, well onto the clear glass on the punty (photo 8). This motion is similar to spreading icing on a cake with a spatula! Continue to swipe encase, adding the white glass all around the cylinder. Each swipe should slightly overlap the previous one, so you don't trap any excess air that will create bubbles (photo 9). After you've encased the entire cylinder, heat the interior and smooth it with the graphite rod. Smooth the exterior by heating it and rolling it gently on a marver (photo 10). Don't press too hard, or the cylinder will collapse.

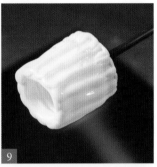

APPLYING THE STRIPES

After the cylinder is smooth, use the intense black stringer to add four stripes equidistant from each other, running the length of the cylinder. To do this, hold the cylinder under the flame in your nondominant hand. Then, holding the stringer in your dominant hand, heat the tip of the stringer and touch it to the clear glass at the base of the cylinder (photo 11). Lay the stringer on the cylinder, and use the radiant heat from the underside of the flame to affix the stringer to the cylinder. The stringer should end at the open edge of the cylinder and should be well affixed to it (photo 12).

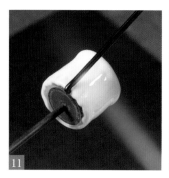

After all four stripes are applied, apply four more, each one about 2 mm away from the first (photo 13). You should have a smooth white cylinder with eight stripes running the length of it (photo 14)

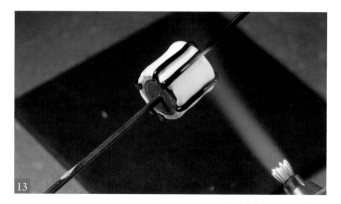

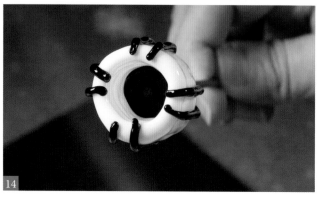

Now make the black stripes twice as deep. Using the same technique, add a second layer of intense black stringer on top of the initial stripes (photo 15). Heat them well, to attach the second layer to the first, but these deep stripes should remain in sharp relief, not melted down into the cylinder. They are the "walls" between which the transparent stripes will flow.

In whichever color scheme you've chosen, prepare a molten gather at the end of the A rod, and then use the swipe-encasing method to stripe that color between two narrowly spaced stripes of black stringer (photo 16); this will result in a narrow transparent stripe on the finished beads.

Repeat this step so that you apply one layer of A in the four narrow gaps around the bead, and then fill the wide gaps with a swipe of the B color (photo 17). Because the black stringer is two layers tall, it's usually necessary to apply a second swipe of the A and then the B color, so that the wall is equally thick all the way around the cylinder.

Take one last opportunity to smooth the exterior of the cylinder and to check that its walls are of a consistent thickness. Then heat only the rim of the open end of the cylinder, and press it gently against a marver to achieve a flat edge at the end of the cylinder. This flat rim will make it easier to attach the second punty. This is also a good time to make sure that the interior of the cylinder is uniform and hasn't collapsed inward anyplace. If it has, heat the cylinder and manipulate it with the graphite rod until the shape is restored.

ATTACHING THE SECOND PUNTY

Keeping the finished cylinder warm in the back of the flame, carefully remove the garaged punty from the kiln, and gradually introduce it to the heat. Try to turn it so that the glass-covered face of the disk becomes molten and glowing (photo 18). When the punty is glowing hot, attach it to the open end of the cylinder (photo 19).

It's very important that there be no gaps between the cylinder and the second punty, so take a moment to carefully survey the new seam between the two. If you see an opening, direct the heat at that spot and angle the cylinder so that the glass flows to fill in the gap (photo 20). The air you've trapped inside the cylinder will form the hole of your tube beads; if it leaks out though a gap, the cylinder will collapse.

PULLING THE TUBE

Hold both punties and the cylinder parallel to the table, and heat the full length of the cylinder as you rotate it in the flame. Try not to heat the center third of the cylinder; instead, direct the flame toward the right and left thirds (photo 21). This will still provide plenty of heat

to the center and enable you to pull the entire cylinder into a long tube, not just the center, reducing the chances of the center collapsing and ruining the central hole.

Remember that this cylinder has thick walls of glass. Instead of ferociously heating one spot, raise the heat base of the entire cylinder a little at a time, adding more and more heat throughout the cylinder. As the cylinder gets hotter and thus soupier, I usually rock it both toward me and away from me, rather than rotate it in a single direction.

When the entire cylinder is molten and you've begun to struggle to keep it from drooping, raise the cylinder above the flame, still rocking it to keep it on center. (Now you'll see why it's helpful to learn this technique with a white-cored cylinder, which turns clear when it's hot but returns to white as it cools down.) Just as the white color begins to return, slowly start to pull the cylinder into a tube. As the glass cools down, pull faster, to make the tube as long as possible (photo 22). The finished tube will be 6 to 7 mm in diameter (photo 23).

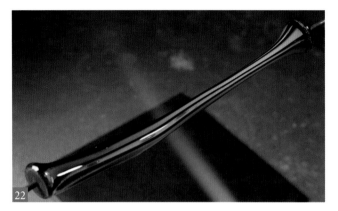

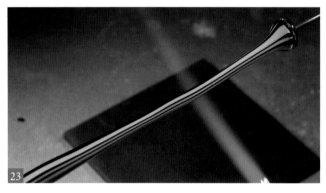

Hint: I sometimes find that it's easier to get an even pull and a good hole if I pull one hand toward the ceiling and one toward the floor.

workshop*wisdom*

It's a good idea to practice pulling tubes with stripes, because the stripes act as visual aids to make sure the cylinder isn't slumping or melting askew. On the other hand, if pulling isn't a challenge for you, try this: as you pull the cylinder into a tube, twist your hands in opposite directions as you would when making a twistie, to add a twist to the surface of your cane. Another variation is to pull the tube with a curve, which means the resulting beads will also curve, perhaps for use in a bracelet.

REMOVING THE PUNTIES

Place the pulled tube on a heatproof surface. In my experience, the cooled glass breaks where it's attached to the punty, making it simple to clean the glass from the steel. If you want to reuse the punties immediately, or even if you just don't have room on your work space for the tube with punties attached, touch the hot glass with a drop of water from a dampened knife or tweezers, which will cause it to fracture. Put the hot punty into water to shock the glass free from the steel. Allow the tube to cool completely.

workshop*wisdom*

Sometimes the cylinder won't pull evenly, and one or both ends will end up fat. One option is to use the fat ends to make fat beads. If you don't like that idea, cut or fracture the tube at the fat point, and re-punty up the open end with any rod you have on hand. If the fat remainder hasn't cooled very much, you should be able to reheat the remainder of the tube and draw it down farther. This can leave you with skinny tubes, but they make great dangles or earring beads.

CUTTING THE BEADS

When the tube is completely cool, use a permanent marker to determine where it should be cut into separate beads. If you have the use of a wet saw (a diamond-encrusted saw blade that has a constant source of water), it's a great tool for cutting beads. Just hold the tube firmly and slowly introduce it into the blade, so that the tube chips as little as possible (photo 24). Always remember to wear eye protection!

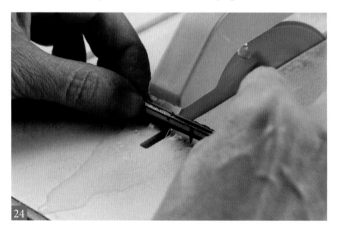

If you don't have a wet saw, score the tube at the marked spot, using a tungsten carbide knife. Dampen the score, hold the tube with your thumbs just on either side of the score, and snap the tube away from your body. After a little practice, this becomes very easy.

FINISHING THE ENDS

One good way to finish the cut ends of these beads is to sand them with wet/dry sandpaper, using first the 170- and then the 600-grit paper. This grinding and polishing could also be done on a belt sander or the flat lap wheel shown in photo 25. Be sure to hold the bead at a good right angle to the grinding surface. If you finish the beads in one of the cold-work methods, batch-anneal them in the kiln after they're sanded.

A color variation or a slight twist in the cane can greatly alter the appearance of the finished bead.

Another way to finish the beads is to put them in a cold kiln, and bring them up to 50° to 100°F (10° to 38°C) hotter than the annealing temperature. Light the torch, use serrated tweezers to remove the beads from the kiln one by one, and fire-polish both ends in the torch. Don't overdo it, or the polished ends will obscure the holes. After fire-polishing, return the beads to the kiln and anneal on the usual schedule. Although this gives the beads a lovely finish, it can be tedious for more than the occasional tube.

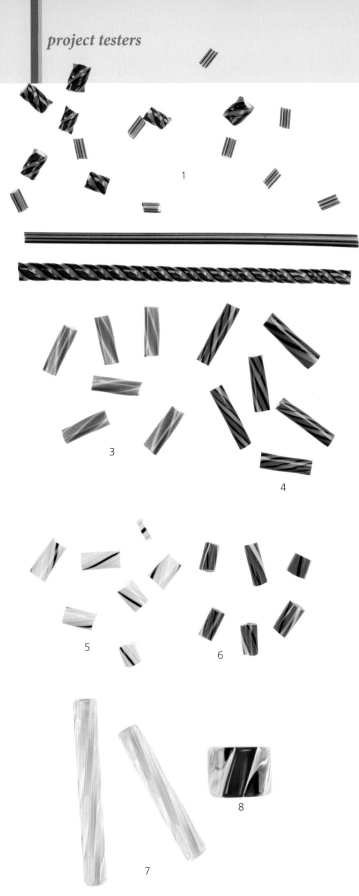

Project Testers

Not every one of the Project Testers had an opportunity to try this project. In our last few months of working together, my spare pair of cabochon mandrels crisscrossed the United States, giving a few more members the chance to pull these tubes. Those who attempted them agreed that the beads are fun, perhaps even addictive, but definitely not a profit center for production beadwork. They take too long to make and use up too much fuel. But did I mention they are *really* fun?

Most group members stayed with techniques and color schemes similar to mine, as Ginny did **(PHOTO 1)**. Others turned out successful versions in an array of colors, some adding an attractive twist to the cane. Note the beads by Ann **(PHOTOS 3 AND 4)**, Sharon **(PHOTOS 5 AND 6)**, and Kristen **(PHOTO 2)**.

Almost everyone found they had to practice a few times to work out the kinks. In particular, the ratio of the thickness of the walls to the diameter of the hole is important; beads that are too thick or pulled too long can end up with very skinny little holes that are impractical for most applications—which is what happened to Ann **(PHOTO 11)**.

Hayley **(PHOTO 10)** was determined to conquer this bead, which she considered far outside her comfort zone. She kept careful track of her journey and reported her progress in an illustrated e-mail:

"The first time I tried it, I followed the directions for wrapping two layers of white. I think it got too thick. I wasn't sure how much to heat the 'ginormous' glob, so I ended up with a fairly big chunk in the middle, which I twisted. Unfortunately, it cracked after one day (and after all the sanding was done!), so I broke the cracked piece off and sanded some more. What I ended up with were two

9

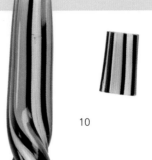

10

11

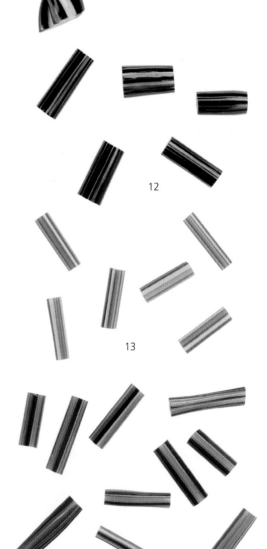

12

13

14

small pieces and one large twisted one—perfect for a pendant and a pair of earrings! I must have had a hard time keeping the glob heated evenly, for the hole is flattened.

"The second time, I tried it with one layer of white and one layer of black. I added more black and thus got a completely different look. Still had trouble pulling the cane evenly. This time I put the cane in the kiln immediately after pulling it, and re-annealed again after sanding. Bead hole looks better—somewhat roundish **(PHOTO 12)**.

"Third try. Instead of intense black (per the original in-structions), I used blue goldstone stringers—one layer of white and one layer of blue goldstone. In addition, I pulled thick stringers of the other colors too, so I could lay the glass down tightly against the blue goldstone. I find that much easier than laying down glass using a full rod. I like the simplicity of these **(PHOTO 13)**.

"Last attempt. One layer of white (I find that works best for me) and two layers of blue goldstone stringers for a thicker look. Again, pulling thick stringers of the other colors was the key in laying them down tight against the 'wall' I built with the blue goldstone. In this case, I used rubino and a silver laden glass that I had received as a test sample. Whew **(PHOTO 14)**!"

Hannah, who had some experience with this type of bead, produced some lovely tubes that were long and slightly curved **(PHOTO 9)**. She uses these as focal pieces in necklaces, embellish-ing them with seed beadwork that wraps around the outside.

Hannah discovered a different approach when learning to make true furnace beads from artist Michael Mangiafico. Es-sentially, she used a mini blowpipe to blow a gather of glass into an optic mold, and then pulled that gather into the tube. Here is her blue furnace glass inspiration bead, alongside the beads she made at the torch **(PHOTOS 7 AND 8)**. Way to go, Hannah!

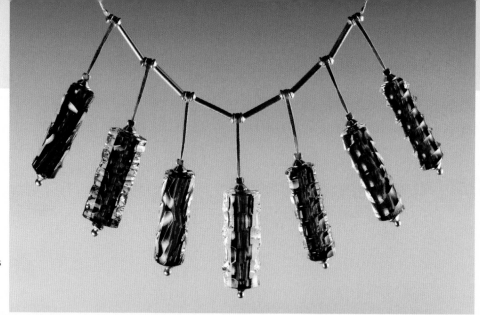

William Glasner
Amethyst Seven-Bead Necklace, 2009
Each bead, approximately 1⅛ x ⅜ x ⅜ inches
    (3 x 1 x 1 cm)
Hand-pulled furnace tubing; wheel carved,
    polished
Photo by artist

Isla Osborne
Felted Pod Necklace, 2009
25 ⅝ x 1⅛ x 1⅛ inches (65 x 3 x 3 cm)
Glass, merino fleece, sterling silver;
    lampworked, wet felted and dyed,
    soldered, constructed
Photo by artist

William Glasner
Carved Aqua Drop, 2009
1⅛ x ¹³⁄₁₆ x ⅜ inches (3 x 2 x 1 cm)
Hand-pulled furnace tubing; wheel
    carved, acid etched
Photo by artist

Larry Scott
Torch-Drawn Tube Beads, 2000–2010
Each, ⅞ x ⅛ x ⅛ inches (2.2 x 0.4 x 0.4 cm)
Soft glass; flameworked
Photo by artist

Joyce Roessler
Blue Frost Necklace, 2006
16 inches (40.6 cm) long
Hand-blown furnace glass; sculpted,
    cut, tumble finished
Photo by George Post

Mary Mullaney and Ralph Mossman
Bead 13, 2004
Largest, 2 x 1 x 1 inches (5 x 2.5 x 2.5 cm)
Soft glass; drawn, cut, ground, polished
Photo by artist

Hannah Rachel Rosner
Harvest, 2009
18 inches (45.7 cm) long
Soft glass; torch blown, cold polished,
    bead woven, wire worked
Photo by artist

Silver
Butterfly

Hot glass and liquid silver are married in this bead to create a surface that can't be achieved any other way.

What Will This Session Teach?

In this project you'll have a chance to practice the basic lentil shape and the use of a bead press. You'll also create a silver design by applying a resist pattern and sandblasting around it.

Glass & Materials

Glass rods **Ⓐ**
  Transparent light teal
  Transparent dark blue
  Transparent dark aqua
  Opaque white
Alcohol wipe **Ⓘ**
Art Clay Silver 650 Overlay Paste **Ⓓ**
Vinyl resist material **Ⓙ**

Tools

Basic hand tools (page 6)
Brass lentil press with flat bottom,
    1¼ inches (3.2 cm) in diameter **Ⓑ**
Mandrel, ¹⁄₁₆ inch (1.6 mm) in diameter,
    or mandrel to fit press
Sandblasting equipment
Shot glass **Ⓒ**
Brush, small **Ⓗ**
Wooden skewer **Ⓖ**
Polishing cloth **Ⓕ**
Scrapbooking punch **Ⓔ** or small scissor
Craft knife

Notes on Tools and Materials

Art Clay Silver 650 Overlay Paste A form of liquefied silver clay, this paste fires to pure silver on the surface of the bead. You don't need to be expert in its use to integrate it into lampwork beads. Because it's used like any other paint, all you need is a small container to dilute the paste and a small, clean brush to apply it to the bead.

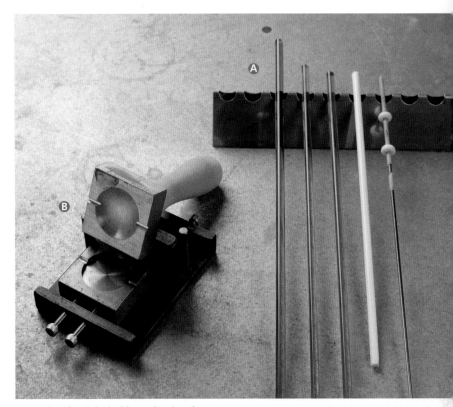

The rod at far right holds marker beads.

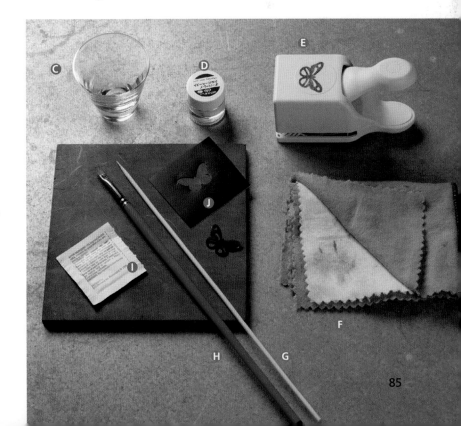

Lentil press Use a lentil press with a flat bottom, if you have one available. If not, this bead can be made in any shape, with adjustments to the design. When firing the silver overlay paste on a bead that's curved on both sides, however, rest the bead on a fiber blanket on the floor of the kiln, to keep it from slumping slightly in the high heat necessary for the silver clay.

Mandrel to fit the press Most commercially available presses are drilled to accept 1/16-inch (1.6 mm) mandrels; other sizes are available only by special order. Keep in mind that if the mandrel is too thick for the press, you're likely to fracture the bead release around the bead when you press the bead into shape.

Brush Sometimes called a *shader*, a small brush with a blunt end will leave as few brush strokes as possible in the dried overlay paste.

An Overview

A flat-backed, lentil-shaped bead lends itself to this project, because it can withstand the heat necessary to fire the overlay paste into fine silver without losing its shape, as a rounder bead might do. The silver sandblasts away easily from around a resist pattern, leaving a silver butterfly in sharp relief.

Creating the Bead

The core of this bead is white, with transparent colors added after the base bead is almost fully shaped. The trick is to make the white core slightly smaller than the size ultimately required for the press, so that after the transparents are added, the bead won't overflow the press cavity.

When using a lentil-shaped brass press, I like the footprint of the bead to be almost exactly the width of the bottom of the cavity. In an effort to reliably repeat this footprint, I've created one mandrel with two spacers that are in the right spot for the footprint of the bead (photo 1). When I begin a new

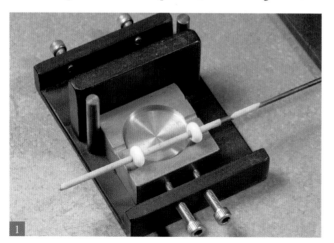

lentil, I align the placement of the first two wraps of glass with the two spacers on my "measurement mandrel," so that I'm assured of the correct overall bead width.

MAKING THE BASE BEAD

Using opaque white, create a base bead with ends that are two wraps of glass tall, and a tube that's filled in between the two ends (photo 2). When this fat tube is finished, wrap on more glass in the center to make an olive shape (photo 3). For most beads, I warn students to keep the heat of the flame away from the bead ends, to preserve the puckered holes. But this time, heat the entire bead. Even though the ends will draw in slightly toward the center, that will be remedied by the final press, which will spread the glass outward.

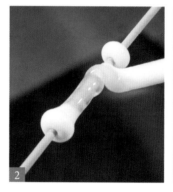

After the olive shape is achieved, the bead is almost large enough to be pressed. Now to add the transparent colors that give the bead its wispy, dreamy appearance. Beginning with the transparent dark blue, form a pea-size molten gather at the end of the rod, and spiral on wraps in several spots around the bead (photo 4). Then spiral on the teal and the aqua, trying to cover the white completely, but also trying to add the transparent glass with a uniform thickness (photo 5). If any areas of white remain uncovered, just dab transparent glass on those spots. To ensure that the white won't show too much around the bead holes, add a skinny little wrap of transparent glass as close to the mandrel as possible, being careful that you're attached to the base bead, not touching the mandrel.

When the white core bead is completely covered by transparent glass, begin to heat the bead to create a smooth surface. Be very careful that you hold the mandrel parallel to the table, so that you keep the bead symmetrical and on center. Sometimes it helps to gently roll the warm bead on a marver to smooth the transparent glass on the surface. To do this without altering the shape of the bead, first allow the core to cool, so it isn't malleable. Then heat the surface of the bead in the flame, and roll it very gently over the marver. Because the core is cooler, touching the surface of the bead won't distort its overall shape.

PRESSING THE BEAD

After the bead is entirely smooth, it's time to begin adding the heat required to press it. Because you'll be working with molten and moving glass, take a moment to assure yourself that the press is in a convenient spot on your bench, with no stray tools to get in your way.

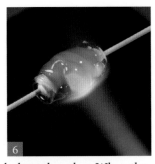

Put the bead in the hottest part of the flame—usually about 2 or 2½ inches (5.1 or 6.4 cm) from the torch head— and rotate the bead slowly so the heat can pour into the very core of the bead (photo 6). Because the bead is slightly wider than the flame, remember to introduce heat into the entire bead, extending from one hole to the other. When the bead is red hot, it's time to move to the press.

The silver butterfly really pops on this purple variation, but the project bead is more challenging because it entails encasing the base bead.

Remove the bead from the flame and, continuing to rotate it, position it over the press. By the time it gets there, the red glow should have subsided, but if it hasn't, pause for a few more seconds (still rotating the bead) until it does. At that moment, put the bead into the bottom of the press and, with your free hand, push the top of the press onto the bead (photos 7 and 8).

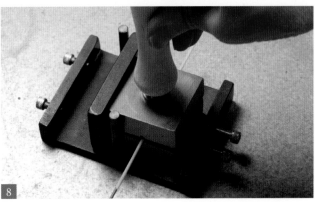

If all goes right, the top will completely close over the bottom, and the cavity will completely fill with glass (photo 9).

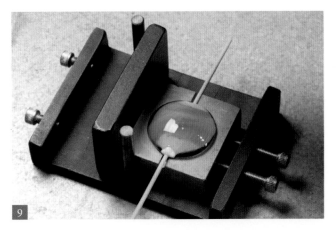

Bring the lentil bead back into the flame, but instead of rotating it, direct the flame at one side of the lentil, bringing that surface to a dull glow (photo 10). Then, while holding the bead just above the flame, turn it so the glowing surface faces the ceiling (photo 11). This will eliminate the circular chill mark left by the metal press. Repeat to remove the chill mark from the opposite surface of the bead. When the chill marks are gone and the bead is evenly warm, it's ready to be annealed.

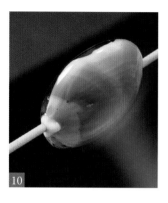

workshop*wisdom*

With enough practice, it's easy to get a good pressed shape every time. But when you're new to presses, or even just new to a press shape, some typical problems can arise. If the base bead is too large, glass will ooze out around the edges of the cavity, and ruin the sharp edge of the lentil. It's usually feasible to return the bead to the flame, heat the edge that extends beyond the lentil shape, and remove the excess glass with pointed tweezers. Don't try to remove too much at one time. Rather, just heat and remove small amounts of glass until you've removed the excess, then reheat the edge and reshape it by using the tip of the press mold as the marver to guide the curve of the desired shape.

If the bead is too small and doesn't completely fill the cavity, try reheating the bead and returning it to the olive base shape. Then add more transparent glass before pressing the bead once again. If the bead is not only too small but also narrower than the width of the lentil (meaning your initial bead footprint wasn't long enough on the mandrel), add glass to the "shoulders" of the bead, 1 to 2 mm in from the hole. This is a more difficult fix, and you should make note of the problem so you can adjust your method for establishing that initial footprint.

APPLYING THE SILVER PASTE

Bead artist Rocio Bearer, who has worked extensively with silver clay, taught me that when you remove the cooled bead from the kiln, you should be careful not to touch it at all. Treat it as though it's been sterilized, and it will have an ideal surface for the application of the silver. More recently, however, I've gotten better silver adhesion by lightly sandblasting the surface of the bead before painting it with silver. (Alternatively, you can dip the bead in etching solution for three to five minutes.) After either of these processes, clean the bead with an alcohol wipe (photo 12).

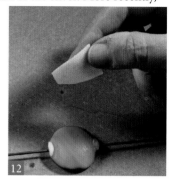

Add water to a small amount of silver overlay paste until it has the consistency of milk (another tip from Rocio). I mix the paste in a shot glass (photo 13). Paint a thin layer of the liquefied paste onto the cooled bead, trying to leave as few brush strokes as possible (photos 14 and 15). Bead artist Beth Williams gave me the helpful suggestion that I dry the wet silver clay under a lamp or on a coffee warmer, to hasten the process.

Allow the silver paste to dry, then fire the bead in the kiln. I typically ramp my kiln up from room temperature to 1200°F (648.9°C) over about 25 minutes. I hold at that temperature for 30 minutes, ramp down to 960°F (515.5°C), and then run the bead through the annealing cycle.

CREATING THE DESIGN

For this bead, I've chosen a simple design that leaves plenty of silver on the surface. Because the silver is pricey, it's silly to use it only to sandblast it away.

To prepare the bead for sandblasting, remove all of the bead release that surrounds the bead, but leave the bead on the mandrel. Then use a clean polishing cloth to wipe the silver surface so it's clean and dry, without any bead release residue or other dirt that would interfere with the adhesion of the resist pattern (photo 16).

workshop*wisdom*

I've made many of these beads (more than I'm willing to reveal) in my efforts to get this technique to work properly. One problem was that the silver tended to be thinner on the center of the lentil and thicker around the edges. (Neil Fabricant, my husband and partner-in-beads, surmised that it flows while still wet.) The thicker edge is harder to sandblast through, and lengthy sandblasting chews up the bead underneath the silver. My solution has been to use a dampened paper towel to wipe clean the outer edge of the lentil before the silver dries, or to scrape away the excess with a wooden skewer after it dries but before firing (photo 17). Remember this tendency to flow and pool, so that you can deal with it if you encounter it in the bead shape you choose.

Use a scrapbooking punch to cut out a mask in the shape of a butterfly from the vinyl resist material. If you don't have a punch, cut a butterfly design out of the vinyl with a sharp craft knife or tiny scissors. (Another good source of resist patterns is stickers that are either metal foil or holographic.) When you have a shape you like, separate the backing from the vinyl, using a craft knife, and being careful not to touch the adhesive surface with your fingers (photo 18). Apply the resist to the bead, and press it on firmly (photo 19).

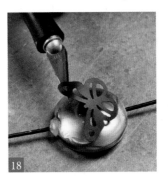

Sandblast the silver surface of the bead to remove all the silver surrounding the vinyl resist (photo 20). Lightly sandblast the flat side of the lentil, so that it has a muted etched surface. Soak the bead in warm water and remove the vinyl (photo 21).

workshop*wisdom*

In my travails developing this bead, at least twice I've removed the vinyl resist only to have the silver come off as well. Clearly, that's a depressing development. I think it's key to paint the silver onto an *absolutely* clean surface, dry it thoroughly, and fire it for the full amount of time and temperature. Realistically, this is still only a thin coating of silver on the surface, so I would consider these beads more delicate than some, and would use them in jewelry where they're protected from frequent battering.

1

2

3

4

5

Project Testers

Although this bead was exciting to the Project Testers, it was also a little intimidating, because it involved an entirely new cold process—the application of silver clay—and access to sandblasting equipment, which no one had. In the end, only an intrepid few finished a version of this bead.

To be fair, this bead is one of the more difficult projects in this book. Even the artist who is a certified silver clay teacher didn't attempt it. Another made her beads, pronounced them "poop," and promptly deposited them in the trash. Even so, three group members ended up with inspiring results.

Ann completed four silvered and sandblasted beads, and in the process overcame common technical challenges. On her three lentil-shaped beads, she painted both sides of the lentil with the Art Clay Silver, something I didn't attempt in the project bead, because it's more difficult to balance and fire the bead without marring the surface. She then successfully masked and sandblasted both sides of each lentil, with positive and negative cutouts of three different images: a frog, a snow-flake, and a leaf **(PHOTOS 2, 3, 4, 8, 9, AND 10)**. Not content with that, she applied a leaf pattern to a long tube bead **(PHOTO 11)**—quite impressive, because it's much trickier to sandblast a curved surface, with its increased risk of "blast-off." (Blast-off occurs when the angled stream of abrasive causes the resist to lift off the surface of the bead, either partially or entirely, resulting in an image that lacks crisp edges.)

Emma completed a rectangular tab bead with a flower ring on one side and a flower pattern on the other **(PHOTOS 6 AND 7)**. On another bead she attempted, when she removed the resist pattern, it took the silver with it. After her experience, I began to lightly sandblast or liquid-etch the beads before applying the silver, which seems to help with adhesion.

6

7

8

9

10

11

Sylvie didn't have access to a sandblaster, but was game to play with the silver overlay paste nonetheless. Her lentils were stamped with rubber stamps, leaving a dreamy, impressionistic effect (PHOTOS 1 AND 5).

Sylvie shared a few tips for her technique of stamping with silver paste:

• It seems to work best if the paste is on the thick side (thicker than pancake batter).

• To use as little paste as possible, apply it with a paintbrush only on the raised part of the rubber stamp.

• Some of the definition of the design is almost always lost, so it's best to pick a simple design with few, if any, intricate details.

• Apply the stamp by pressing firmly.

• When the paste is dry, correct the design as necessary by using a dry ink brush or pen to remove excess silver.

Sylvie observed, "The good thing about doing it this way is that you can wipe the paste off the base bead as many times as you want until you're happy with the result. Of course, you're 'wasting' silver paste, but you don't have to throw away a bead that has been 'ruined' by your first stamping attempts."

Sylvie finished her beads by annealing and then buffing them with a jewelry cloth to bring out the shine of the silver.

After the Project Testers were done with this project, I wanted to try a more complex design, to see whether this project was just unreasonably difficult. I'm happy with this purple lentil (PHOTO 12), and although I think that this bead involves learning lots of new information, the result is very worthwhile.

12

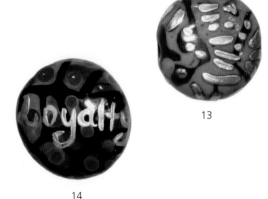

13

14

Emma Mullins, 13, 14

Beth Williams
Silver-Lined Open Hearts, 2007
1⅜ x 1⅛ x ⅜ inches
(3.6 x 3 x 1 cm)
Soft glass; lampworked, selective metal clay application
Photo by Clark Linehan

Barbara Becker Simon
Painted Beads, 2010
Each, 1 inch (2.5 cm) in diameter
Soft glass, metal clay paste; flameworked, painted
Photo by Babette Belmondo

Barbara Becker Simon
Teal Snake Bead, 2006
1⅜ x ⅜ inches (3.5 x 1 cm)
Soft glass, fine silver metal clay
Photo by Robert Diamante

Sharon Peters
The Beagle Has Landed, 2009
2 x 2⅛ x 1¼ inches (5 x 5.5 x 3.2 cm)
Soft glass, steel inclusions; flameworked, electroformed
Photo by Jim Trenkle

Claudia Trimbur-Pagel
Butterflies, 2009
1⅜ x ¾ inches (3.5 x 1.8 cm)
Soft glass, metal clay; sandblasted
Photo by artist

Rocio Bearer
Playful Spring, 2009
2 x 1 x ⅜ inches (5 x 2.6 x 1 cm)
Soft glass, metal clay; flameworked
Photo by artist

Rocio Bearer
Precious Reaction, 2009
1½ x 1½ x ½ inches (3.9 x 3.7 x 1.2 cm)
Soft glass, metal clay; flameworked
Photo by artist

Glass
Memento

Everyone who sees this
pendant puzzles over how I
preserved the image under
what appears to be glass.
(Hint: It's actually resin.)

What Will This Session Teach?

This session introduces the large and heavy big-hole mandrel (a.k.a. *ring mandrel*) and teaches you to apply glass in a novel area: on the end of said mandrel. You'll make a bead using two mandrels at once, experiment with resin, and play with the ruffling pliers—again!

Glass & Materials

Glass rods **D**
> Transparent medium amethyst
> Transparent light amethyst
> Transparent red

Extra-strong bead release

Photo, artwork, or collage materials (see Appendix B, page 134)

Resin (see Appendix B, page 134)

Tools

Basic hand tools (page 6)

Mandrel, short, ³⁄₃₂ inch (2 mm) in diameter, 8 to 9 inches (20.3 to 22.9 cm) long **B**

Ring mandrel, ¾ to 1 inch (1.9 to 2.5 cm) in diameter **A**

Ruffling pliers (page 16) **C**

Notes on Tools and Materials

Extra-strong bead release Most beadmakers develop a fondness for a particular brand of bead release. There are many on the market, and they have different selling features, such as whether they dry in the flame, or whether they're easy to clean from the bead hole. For this bead, choose a bead release that offers you the best possible gripping strength. In particular, if you're using a flat-ended mandrel, you'll need the extra strength to keep the bezel attached to the mandrel while you're working on the pendant.

Resin You'll need either UV (ultraviolet) resin or one of the new two-part resins marketed for craft projects. See Appendix B on page 134 for an extensive discussion.

Mandrel, ³⁄₃₂ inch (2 mm) in diameter and 8 to 9 inches (20.3 to 22.9 cm) in length For me, this is a *short* mandrel; mine are usually 12 inches (30.5 cm) long. The back of the pendant will be made on this mandrel, and later attached to the finished piece. The entire pendant will go into the kiln attached to two mandrels (think two sides of a triangle), and they fit more easily if the back is wound on this short mandrel.

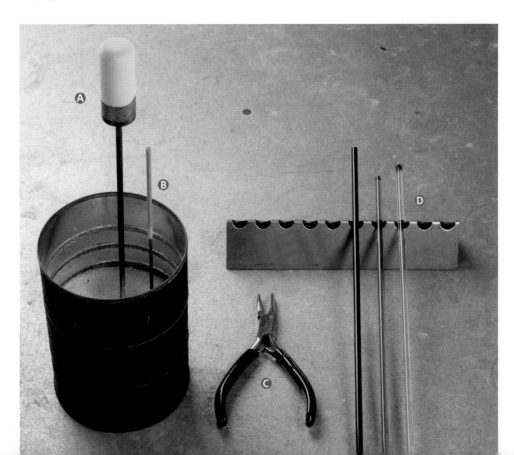

Ring mandrel These comparatively fat mandrels are used in the construction of rings. For this pendant I use one that's ¾ inch (1.9 cm) in diameter, but a mandrel 1 inch (2.5 cm) in diameter works equally well. Ideally, search for one with a tip that's flat rather than convex. The end of the mandrel forms the base, or floor, of the bezel cup, and the resin is much easier to work with if the base is flat. A convex mandrel tip will create a concave bezel cup. This isn't an insurmountable problem, and solutions are discussed below in the Workshop Wisdom box. Scuff the surface of a new mandrel with sandpaper or a steel pad so that it has some "tooth" to grab on to the bead release.

Ruffling pliers This project offers another excuse to use the ruffling pliers, which I adore. (They're described in Session 1—the Ruffled Pendant—on page 16.) Alternatively, any pinching tool will yield good results, including non-serrated tweezers or tungsten tweezers, which are less likely to stick to the glass (photo 1).

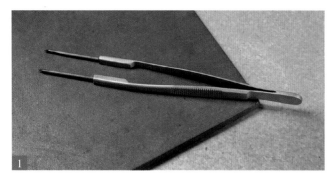

An Overview

This pendant borrows the concept of a *bezel cup* from the jewelry world. Normally, a bezel is made of metal and holds a precious or semiprecious stone or a flat cabochon. In our case, the bezel cup is made of glass and holds glasslike resin, which confounds the viewer and allows the use of fragile components that aren't durable enough for the flame.

> ### workshop*wisdom*
>
> If the only ring mandrel you can find has a convex tip, you can grind it down to a less pronounced curve, or even flat, if you have a grinding wheel. The good news about a convex-end mandrel is that it's slightly easier to use—the glass bezel is less likely to drop off the mandrel while under construction—so perhaps it's a good trade-off for your resin trouble.

When I first laboriously constructed a glass bezel—partly off mandrel and partly on a ring mandrel—I struggled with a lack of symmetry in the finished piece. Beadmaker Susan Lambert suggested I try creating the bezel on the *end* of the ring mandrel, and that transformed my approach to this pendant. When toolmaker Craig Milliron made me some ring mandrels with slightly flattened ends, I was off and running.

Creating the Bead
MAKING THE BAIL

The bail of this pendant—which is essentially a flattened tube bead—is created on the short mandrel. Wind the transparent medium amethyst glass onto the mandrel to create a tube that's ¾ inch (1.9 cm) long (photo 2). Flatten opposing sides of the tube using parallel mashers (photo 3). Don't worry about removing any chill marks on the glass, because you'll reheat this bead when attaching it to the pendant, and the marks will disappear. Put the finished bead into the kiln at annealing temperature, to keep it warm until you're ready for it. (Be careful to leave the majority of the mandrel sticking out so it doesn't get too hot to hold when you remove it.)

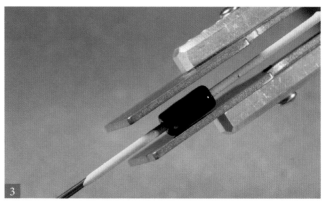

MAKING THE BEZEL WALL

The challenging part of this pendant is to wind an even wrap of glass around the ring mandrel very close to the end. This wrap will form the wall of the bezel—with luck and practice, a wall of uniform width.

Thoroughly preheat the bead release all the way around the ring mandrel, to assure that the glass will adhere to it. Because the entire bezel is attached to the very tip of the mandrel—a somewhat precarious arrangement—the bezel has a tendency to drop off later in the process, while you're ruffling the pendant.

To begin the bezel wall, heat the transparent medium amethyst rod to create a *large* gather. One of the primary problems students encounter is making the wall too narrow in some spots, usually where the wrap of glass begins or ends. To remedy this, make the gather larger than required for a single wrap.

As the gather grows, rock the glass rod toward you and away from you (or in complete rotations) to keep the gather balanced and centered on the rod and prevent it from drooping. When the gather is about the size of a large grape, hold it just above the flame (continuing to rock), so it's less soupy but still hot. A slight skin forms on the gather when you remove it from the flame; it's that skin that keeps the whole wad of glass from landing on the mandrel all at once.

To wind on the glass, position the ring mandrel just below the flame. Make sure the mandrel is rotating *away* from you before you touch the glass to the mandrel. Heat the tip of the gather and touch it to the turning mandrel, at right angles to the mandrel and directly through the flame (or, if your torch is very hot, along the side of the flame). This is shown in photo 4. As the gather reheats through its skin and begins to

workshop*wisdom*

It's easier to balance a large gather on the end of a glass rod if you tip the cold end of the rod toward the table, keeping the hot end in the flame. The tipped rod provides a base for the gather; the whole thing will resemble a mushroom cap (the gather) on a mushroom stem (the rod). (As an aside, this is visible in photo 7, on page 98.)

flow down onto the mandrel more quickly, control the width of the wrap of glass by positioning the mandrel farther from the flame, closer to the work surface (photo 5). Never stop turning the mandrel.

To end the wrap, stretch the mandrel and the gather even farther apart (move the gather toward your nose and the mandrel toward the work surface), and allow the flame to cut through the connection. Again, it remains important that you continue to rotate the ring mandrel so that your wrap ends with a taper, not a lump of glass.

Although this process of winding on the glass took six paragraphs to describe, it takes no longer to *do* than a medium-size spacer bead. Mostly it takes practice to get all the elements in sync: the heat of the bead release, the size and temperature of the gather, the placement of the mandrel and the gather, and the rate of the rotation. If you don't get it exactly right on the first few tries, the pendants will still look good. But it will be hard to finish a piece with a nice, even dome of resin if the bezel wall isn't one consistent width.

After applying an even wrap of glass to the entire circumference of the mandrel, heat the wrap and roll it on a marver so that it spreads to about one and a half times its original width. In the completed bead, the bezel cup should be about ¼ inch (6 mm) deep (photo 6).

MAKING THE BEZEL FLOOR

Keeping the bezel walls warm, create another large gather—again, about the size of a large grape—on the end of the medium amethyst rod (photo 7). When the gather is molten, hold the mandrel at right angles to the flame and just adjacent to it, and press the molten gather onto the flat end of the ring mandrel (photo 8). Detach the rod, using the heat of the flame, and press the gather flat on a marver so it spreads and overlaps the edge of the bezel walls (photo 9).

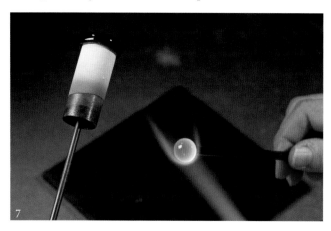

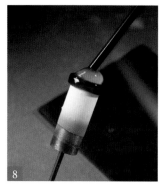

Use heat and the marver to make sure that the bottom of the bezel is flat, that the walls remain flattened (as you heat them they tend to round up), and that there's an invisible seam between the walls and the floor. Add more glass to close the seam if necessary (photo 10). Typically, the bezel walls are ¼ inch (6 mm) wide, and the bottom of the bezel adds about another ¼ inch (6 mm).

MAKING THE HEART SHAPE

To begin the heart, create a gather on the end of the light amethyst rod, and touch it to the rim of the bezel floor, just to one side of the 12 o'clock position. Wind that gather all the way around the rim, until it's about ¼ inch (6 mm) away from the starting point, and then disconnect the rod. This is the inner color of the heart (photo 11). This wrap should remain in relief, not melted down onto the bezel, because it will be pinched to form part of the ruffle. Add a little dot of light amethyst to the bottom of the heart, at about 6 o'clock (photo 12). (*Note*: For easier handling, I'm holding the pendant upside down in the photo, but the dot really is at 6 o'clock. Trust me.)

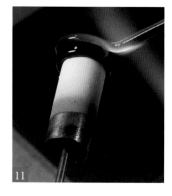

Use the transparent red glass to add two more wraps on top of the light amethyst (photo 13). For each wrap, begin a little farther away from 12 o'clock than the previous wrap (photo 14). After two applications of red, add a little more red glass to the tip of the heart, at 6 o'clock. You should now have a rough heart shape.

The wraps should be attached to the rim of the bezel floor, not to its walls. The flat bottom should join seamlessly with the wraps. Be sure to add enough heat so the wraps are well attached to the base and to each other.

If you don't quite see a heart forming, fatten the lobes by striping on a little more glass. The pendant expands when the ruffle is squeezed, so try not to go overboard with shaping and adding glass at this stage.

ADDING THE RUFFLE
To create the ruffle, spot-heat both the front and the back of one area of the wraps, covering about ½ inch (1.3 cm) at a time, and then use the ruffling pliers to squeeze that spot rapidly, two or three times, before it cools (photo 15). Heat and squeeze the entire heart in this manner (photo 16). I usually do this symmetrically: if I heat and squeeze the top of one lobe of the heart, I do the top of the other lobe next. This helps me see the heart shape begin to emerge and allows me to squeeze less in the areas that will taper equally on both sides, near the tip of the heart.

When you're pleased with the heart shape, take a moment to make certain the back of the pendant is completely flat. This will be important when adding the resin, because it's easier to fill the pendant if it's level. Also check that the ruffled wraps are well adhered to each other, and give one last visual assessment of the symmetry of the bead. This is your last chance to tweak the shape. If you like what you see, move on.

ATTACHING THE BAIL
Keeping the pendant warm in the back of the flame, carefully remove the tube bead from the kiln. Gingerly introduce the tube to the back of the flame (which is hotter than the kiln), and give it a thorough rewarming before moving it into the hotter regions of the flame. The goal here is to get the entire tube hot but not molten. Remember to keep the pendant warm all this time.

To attach the tube to the pendant, begin to heat both the upper half of the pendant's back and one flat side of the tube. This is tricky. Because the ring mandrel is heavy, it's hard to keep the flat back of the pendant in the path of the flame. When the flat side of the tube and the back of the pendant are equally hot and beginning to glow, you're ready to attach the tube to the pendant.

Decide whether you want the heart to hang at an angle or straight up and down, because the bail will control the way the pendant hangs. Make sure the tube bail doesn't show above the edge of the bezel. Give one last reheating to the flat surface of the tube and to the back of the pendant to bring them to a glow, and press the flat side of the tube onto the bottom of the bezel. Talk about awkward! Now you have one pendant with *two* mandrels. Give everything one last dose of heat, especially the ruffle, and pop the assemblage in the kiln to anneal (photo 17).

ADDING THE INCLUSIONS

After the bead is annealed and thoroughly cleaned of bead release, insert the image of your choice into the bottom of the bezel. Cover the image with resin, and allow it to cure. (See Appendix B, Working with Resin, on page 134.)

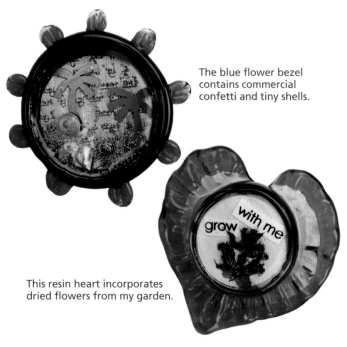

The blue flower bezel contains commercial confetti and tiny shells.

This resin heart incorporates dried flowers from my garden.

workshop*wisdom*

There are two junctures at which the pendant tends to fall off the ring mandrel: when ruffling the heart, and when attaching the bail. This isn't fatal. If the pendant falls off during ruffling, pick it up from the work surface, using either the ruffling pliers or the tweezers (photo 18). Grab any rod on your bench and, while keeping the bezel warm in the back of your flame, create a gather on the rod, and stick it to the bead release inside the bezel cup (photo 19). This rod becomes the new "handle" for working on the pendant. It will easily release when the bead is cooled, because it's attached to the bead release, not the glass interior of the pendant. You can also remove it by cutting it with the flame before putting the pendant in the kiln (photo 20). Next time, avoid torquing the ruffle with the pliers, which is what pulls the pendant from the mandrel.

If the pendant falls off the mandrel after the tube bead is applied, just give the whole thing one last reheating—supporting the entire pendant by holding the tube bead's mandrel—and put it in the kiln. Sometimes, even when the pendant goes in the kiln attached to both mandrels, the ring mandrel drops out during annealing, and no harm is done. Always stay sensitive to the fact that there just isn't much contact between the bezel and the bead release, so the glass doesn't have a lot to hang on to.

1

2

Project Testers

For this bead, the Project Testers included two "ringers": artists who had played with plenty of resin. My everlasting gratitude goes out to Sharon and Jen, who were among my resin consultants. The entire group benefited from their experience, as we swapped e-mails while working on these beads.

Jen makes pins and ornaments that include metal bottle caps as elements of the design, and she fills the bottle caps with tiny images that are covered in resin. She suggested on-line photo resources as a source of copyright-free photos and images. Sharon, who makes pendants that incorporate resin images, also suggested on-line craft sites where artists sell "inchies." These are images about 1 inch (2.5 cm) square that can be downloaded to mobile media for printing at a commercial printer, or on your own color printer. Taking another approach, Sharon drew the sun with indelible marker and color pencils **(PHOTO 18)**. I enjoy cutting up the images in old calendars and maps. I also like to print color photos in sepia or black and white, and use those photos in my collages.

All of the artists struggled with getting a nice even rim to the bezel. Jen finished one of hers with a twistie, thus masking any unevenness. (Clever Jen.) The simple floral image echoes the color scheme of the decorated reverse side **(PHOTOS 1 AND 2)**.

Sharon took a different approach to the two-sided design, opting for contrast instead of thematic colors. On one side she encased a Day of the Dead image, while on the reverse she placed an innocent little flower **(PHOTOS 3 AND 4)**. Sharon also made a pendant bezel that could be strung through the top loop and embellished with a dangle on the lower loop. It too has a decorated reverse side, which she says can be worn like a locket, with a personal image against the wearer's body and the decorated reverse worn like any lovely pendant **(PHOTOS 5 AND 6)**.

Group members who were trying resin for the first time found it surprisingly easy, whether they used a two-part resin or

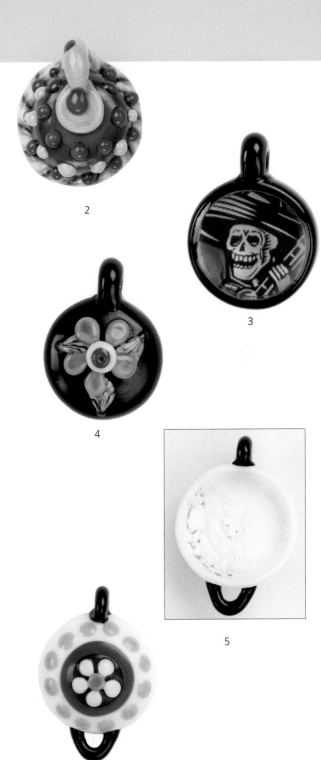

3

4

5

6

7

8

9

10

11

12

one that was light-cured. Hayley made a flower with a loop bail behind one petal. The small bubble that remained in the resin became part of the design. Hayley thinks the bubble resulted from the paper image not being completely flat within the bezel, thus trapping a bit of air **(PHOTO 7)**. One solution is to use resin that's self-leveling (such as light-cured resin) and to put a tiny floor of cured resin in the bottom of the bezel before adding the paper. Another idea is to glue the sealed image to the bottom of the bezel, using white glue.

Although the resin was easy, construction offered its usual challenges. Ann found that when she attached the tube-shaped bail to the back of the main bead, one bead or the other broke loose from the bead release. She thinks she might prefer making the tube bead in advance, then bringing it up to temperature in the kiln and attaching it to the finished bezel with tweezers. This would eliminate the dual mandrels, which can be a tight fit in the kiln. Like Jen, Ann also used a twistie in her puppy bead to conceal an uneven edge **(PHOTOS 11 AND 12)**. In the future, she plans to try making the rim of the bezel with a fat stringer, instead of a rod.

Debby totally eliminated the need for two mandrels by making her beads as pins. After the resin cups were filled and cured, she glued metal pin backs on her pieces, using a silicone-based glue. Her diverse and wonderful collages include micro beads in the bottom of each cup **(PHOTOS 13, 14, AND 15)**.

Finally, Jen and Sharon also strategized bezels that didn't require that second mandrel. Jen solved the problem with copper wire loops, embedded in the glass at the torch. She filled her piece with a vintage button **(PHOTO 8)**. Sharon created this vintage fairy piece as a rim around a mandrel, with no base. To fill it with resin, she adhered the ring to clear packing tape and then used a little bit of glitter mixed into the resin to obscure any cloudiness left when the tape was removed. This see-through resin piece has a glass loop at the top **(PHOTO 9)**.

13

14

15

Everyone agreed that this project had both possibilities and challenges. Grinding the concave end of the ring mandrel to slightly flatten it (as I do) makes for a bezel cup that is easier to use, because the interior is flat. *But* everyone had the occasional bezel drop off, because it's much harder to have retention with a flat mandrel. Debby didn't own any ring mandrels, but wasn't deterred. She stuffed the end of her large tube mandrel with steel wool, then coated it in three or four layers of bead release, which she gently rubbed smooth in between applications (photo below). She adapted this from a well-known technique for making core-formed vessels. The group was excited about this possibility, because it meant the bezels didn't need to be round. This same method would be fun to try on any tube mandrels, such as the oval or heart-shaped ones.

16

17

18

Ann Conlin, **16, 17**; Sharon Driscoll, **10**

103

Jennifer Place
Necklace for Violet, 2010
4 x 10 inches (10.2 x 25.4 cm)
Soft glass, stainless steel loops, bezels, buttons, photo,
    locket, coin, earring, sterling silver chain; flameworked
Photo by artist

Ann Scherm Baldwin
Time Machine, 2010
2⅜ x 1 x ⅝ inches (6 x 2.5 x 1.5 cm)
Soft glass, resin, watch parts, image;
    lampworked
Photo by David L. Totten

Ann Scherm Baldwin
Expecting Evelyn, 2010
1⅛ x 1 x ⅝ inches (3 x 2.5 x 1.5 cm)
Soft glass, resin, image; lampworked
Photo by David L. Totten

Eleanore Macnish
Pendant for Alice…in Wonderland, 2010
Pendant, 3½ x 2⅜ inches (9 x 6 cm)
Glass bead, sterling silver, vintage glass rose,
    vintage mother of pearl button; lampworked,
    soldered, sawed, bezel set
Photo by artist

Susan Walter
Untitled, 2010
2¾ x 2 x ⅜ inches (7 x 5 x 1 cm)
Soft glass, resin inlay; flameworked
Photo by Phillip Rout

Susan Walter
Untitled, 2010
2⅛ x 1⅞ x ⅜ inches (5.5 x 4.5 x 1 cm)
Soft glass, resin inlay; flameworked
Photo by Phillip Rout

Susan Lambert
Pulp Fiction, 2010
1⅛ inches (3 cm)
Soft glass, resin
Photo by artist

Susan Lambert
Graffiti, 2010
1⅜ inches (3.5 cm)
Soft glass, resin
Photo by artist

Glass Portal

This time-consuming bead is a labor of love. The resulting piece is a novel view of a bead, wearable alone as a pendant or as part of a great assemblage.

What Will This Session Teach?

Here you'll learn how to double-encase a hollow bead, a task made easier when using the Puffy Mandrel. This bead also provides a canvas for exploring enamel and reduction frit. Finally, you'll use a flat lap grinder to expose the interior of the bead.

Glass & Materials
Glass rods **C**
> Transparent light aqua
> Transparent dark aqua
> Transparent olive green

Enamel, white (page 38) **B**

Frit, aqua, medium (page 26) **E**

Reduction frit, silver green, medium (page 37) **F**

Tools
Basic hand tools (page 6)

Puffy Mandrel, ³⁄₃₂ inch (2 mm) in diameter (page 63) **A**

Enamel sifter **B**

Tungsten pick or other metal pick **D**

Flat lap grinder

Polishing machine

Rag buffing wheel

Cerium oxide

Notes on Tools and Materials

Enamel In Session 3, we applied enamel to the Eye Bead by rolling the hot bead in powdered enamel (see page 41). For this project, we'll use a basket sifter.

Enamel sifter The newest style has a metal sleeve that can slide along the handle and cause the basket to "shiver."

Tungsten pick Unlike steel, tungsten resists sticking to hot glass, which is important in making this bead.

Flat lap grinder The ground and polished surfaces of this bead are achieved by grinding the glass on successively finer grinding disks and then polishing the bead with cerium oxide.

Overview

This pendant makes a novel use of the hollow bead form. The appeal of a hollow bead usually comes from its deceptive lightness. Here, the holes of a thickly encased hollow bead are sliced away to reveal the portal in the center, surrounded by thick, striated walls. The thin slice is then ground and polished to a shiny finish.

Creating the Bead
HOLLOW BEAD PHYSICS

Typically, a hollow bead is made from two disks built a short distance apart, then either bent or coiled toward each other and seamed together. When the seamed bead is heated, the air trapped inside expands, inflating the bead.

For this to work, the disks must be as thin as possible. Otherwise, their weight will collapse the bead as it rounds and inflates. The pitfall is that thin disks are hard to create and harder to keep warm. A thin disk loses its heat very quickly and is shockier than a thick one.

It's easier to build a hollow bead around the pierced hole in a Puffy Mandrel, because the disks don't have to be ultra-thin. Ultimately, the bead is inflated both by the traditional method (the warming of the interior air) *and* by blowing additional air through the mandrel and directly into the bead. That's important for this bead, because its walls are triple-thick and thus more susceptible to collapse from sheer weight.

---

workshop*wisdom*

If your initial wrap of glass on the mandrel tends to be uneven in width—wide in spots or skinny in spots—there are various ways to prevent that from happening.

Too wide? Make a large gather, let it cool for a second or two, then touch it to the mandrel with the tiniest connection possible. If this is hard to do with a stiffening gather, then after the large gather has slightly cooled, reheat just the tip of it before touching it to the mandrel. This will help avoid a wide spot caused by mashing too much of the gather onto the mandrel at the start of the wrap.

Too skinny? Use a large enough gather that some of it is left behind, attached to the rod, when you detach. This will remedy a skinny spot resulting from having too little molten glass to complete that first wrap. After you prepare a gather, try wrapping the bead just below the flame, with the rod at right angles to the bead and passing through the flame. This enables you to stop after a single wrap or to have a continuous supply of molten glass to make the bead larger.

A blob? If your bead ends with a blob, remember to roll the bead away from you, and detach the rod by pulling it toward your nose; that will taper the last bit of glass into a skinny wrap.

BUILDING THE HOLLOW BEAD

To begin, wind two spacer beads of the light aqua glass on either side of the pierced hole in the Puffy Mandrel. The beads should be 1 to 1¼ inches (2.5 to 3.2 cm) apart. Those initial spacers provide the footprint for the finished hollow bead. If they're a little too fat, that won't be a problem for this bead.

Build the disks on top of these two spacers with wraps of about the same width. I usually add one wrap at a time to each disk, warming after each addition of glass (photo 1).

When the disks are about ½ inch (1.3 cm) in diameter, begin coiling them in the direction of each other, meeting more or less in the middle (photo 2). Most beadmakers are more comfortable coiling from one side than the other (maybe this depends on whether you are right- or left-handed), so the seaming of the two sides may be a little to the right or left of center. This won't matter.

Up to this point, the bead is no different from a traditional hollow bead (photo 3). (Maybe a little lumpy and out of round.)

3

INFLATING THE BEAD

To smooth the coils of glass and inflate the hollow bead, slowly rotate and heat the bead in the flame *while keeping your palm or a finger gently over the hole in the undipped end of the mandrel.* Blocking that hole will prevent the warm air inside from escaping out the end of the mandrel and collapsing the bead. I find it easier to hold the mandrel with both hands to the right of the flame (photo 4). If you work slowly, any pinholes will become obvious—they'll be those spots on the bead that aren't getting round—and you can save the bead by closing each hole with a *tiny* dot of glass.

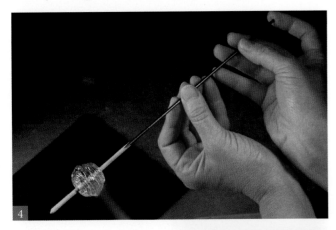

4

Even though you're doing everything right, the bead will collapse inward a little. Don't panic! Continue to heat the bead gently and slowly, because for the next step you'll need an even heat base established throughout the bead (photo 5).

5

workshop*wisdom*

If a disk shocks into pieces when you re-introduce it to the flame, the wraps of glass probably weren't adhered to each other. This is a heat problem. To fix it, remember to heat the outer edge of the disk before adding the next molten wrap, which will ensure a good connection.

Pinholes are another heat-related problem. If the coils in an area look like little inchworms, you've probably added glass that wasn't hot enough, so it didn't flow and make good contact with the rim of the disk. Try working with a hotter gather. I like to feed the rod directly through the flame, with the outer edge of the disk just below the flame.

Keeping the bead parallel to the table, and slowly rotating the mandrel to keep the bead on center, bring the undipped end of the mandrel up to your lip and block the hole by gently pressing the mandrel against your lip. Slowly rotate the mandrel until the bead has just lost its glow. (It sometimes helps to wet your lips so the tube will slide easily.)

Send a gentle puff or two of air into the tube, and then block it again with your lip. You'll see the bead inflate! Of course, because the glass is soft enough to inflate, it's soft enough to droop off-center, so you must keep rotating the bead until it's firm.

Because the bead is about to be doubly encased, the point of inflating it is to make sure it's round and symmetrical, not to greatly increase its size. This bead will grow quite enough as it's encased.

workshop*wisdom*

If the walls of your hollow bead are uneven in thickness, when you inflate it with a puff of air, one spot may expand more rapidly, indicating a thin spot. Don't direct the flame at that spot; it's prone to popping open. Instead, use a molten gather of the same color and swipe a little glass over that spot. This isn't a great fix for a regular hollow, because it creates a thick spot that won't inflate evenly. For this bead, however, it will work. The true solution, of course, is more practice at making disks of even thickness.

ADDING THE ENAMEL

After the light aqua hollow bead is finished—meaning it's sealed, smoothed, and inflated—warm it gently, to prepare the surface for the application of enamel. The bead shouldn't get so hot that it's glowing red or in danger of collapsing, so you don't have to worry about covering the open end of the mandrel.

Hold the bead directly over the enamel container, and use the sifter to cover the surface with white enamel (photo 6). If the enamel doesn't stick, you haven't prewarmed the bead enough. Just heat it again and re-apply the enamel. The goal is an even coat of white that obscures the light aqua glass (photo 7). Once the enamel is adhered, there's no need to reheat it in order to smooth the surface. The enamel will become smooth as additional layers of glass are applied.

ENCASING THE BEAD

The next layer of glass is olive green, which will completely cover the enamel surface over the center three-quarters of the bead. Once again, as in the Cosmic Bead on page 56, we will use "swipe encasing."

Heat a large gather at the end of the olive green rod, a little bigger than a fat pea. Position the bead directly under or behind the flame, with the rod at right angles to the bead, directly through the flame. As you touch the gather to the bead, imagine you're using a spatula to spread icing on a cake, with the gather as the icing and the stiff glass rod as the spatula (photos 8 and 9). When you run out of molten glass, form another gather and continue where you left off, with each new gather just slightly overlapping where the last one ended. Each ring of encasing should be just on the edge of the previous ring. Continue until the center three-quarters of the bead is entirely covered, all the way around the bead's equator (photo 10).

Heat the olive green glass until the outer surface is smooth. This layer doesn't need to be melted flush with the enamel-covered light aqua layer; it just needs to be without bumps.

> ### workshop*wisdom*
> If long, thin bubbles form in the outer encasing of glass as you heat it to smooth it, you've left small gaps between the swipes of glass, rather than overlapping them. As the wraps melt, they trap those long, thin bubbles. Those bubbles will be problematic in the grinding stage, and you should take the time to eliminate them. Find out how in the Workshop Wisdom box on page 57.

To bring this about, focus the flame on the olive green as you rotate the bead, trying not to heat the glass around the mandrel; the bead is thinner there, and too much heat will encourage it to collapse. The advantage of the Puffy Mandrel comes into play here. If the bead gets soft and the least bit wobbly, re-inflate it so it doesn't collapse. The worst-case scenario is if any part of the interior bead walls touches the mandrel, because that will prevent the bead from being entirely hollow.

THE FINAL ENCASING

After the olive green glass is smooth, add a layer of white enamel, just like the enamel on the light aqua layer (photo 11). Finally, using the ever-popular swipe-encasing technique, encase the center three-quarters of the bead with dark aqua (photo 12). Smooth the layer but avoid collapsing the bead, adding puffs of air as necessary.

MAKING THE FUNNELS

The funnels in the concentric layers of the finished bead are caused by plunging the tungsten pick into the outer layer of the bead and forcing the pick toward the mandrel.

Gently warm the entire bead, because you're about to ignore it while using the pick. Spot-heat a single location on the part of the bead that's double-encased. Keep in mind that you need the heat to travel through three thick layers of glass (photo 13). When the spot is molten, move the bead out of the flame, and poke the tungsten pick into the bead, pushing the outer layers into the interior of the bead, toward the mandrel (photo 14). While the glass is still moving, wiggle the pick to enlarge the hole. How far you plunge the pick is up to you, but I like to plunge three spots, and I try to vary the depths of the holes. Make these holes close to the equator, so that you don't grind them away when you finish the bead.

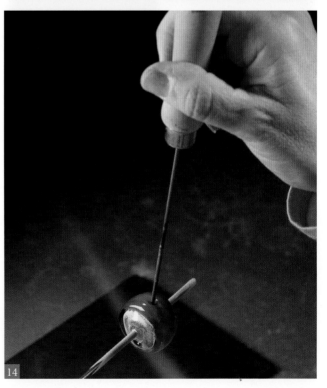

ADDING THE FRIT

Rewarm the outer surface of the bead, just short of a glow, and touch it down into a dish of frit (photo 15). I use primarily aqua frit, with a little pinch of the silver green mixed in. After the frit is stuck to the surface of the bead, warm it again to make sure it's well adhered (photo 16). Finally, bathe the bead in a reduction flame—a flame starved for oxygen—to bring out the metal oxides and give a metallic sheen to the silver green frit (photo 17). The hot part of this bead is now over!

GRINDING AND POLISHING

When the bead is cool, soak the bead and mandrel in warm water until the bead comes off easily. Don't bother cleaning out the bead release.

Now it's time to grind and polish the bead, using the flat lap grinder. For the first cuts, use a grinding wheel with a very abrasive surface, either 100 or 170 grit. This coarse wheel will quickly grind away the useless portions of the bead.

With the grinder running and well lubricated with a flow of water, hold the bead tightly in two hands, and begin to grind it by placing one hole directly down onto the grinding disk. To stay oriented, remember that the bead is in the right position when the remaining (opposite) hole is facing the ceiling.

Grind until all of the unencased light aqua glass is removed and you're just starting to nibble at the double-encased center portion of the bead. Now is a great time to rinse out whatever bead release remains inside the bead.

Turn the bead over, place the second hole against the grinding surface, and grind away the unencased light aqua on the second side. If you were careful to plunge your pick only into the double-encased part of the bead, you should now see the beginning of the interior design, before you've ground away any part of the funnels.

Press the bead against the grinding disk, using only the pressure necessary to hang on to it—no more. Using your own aesthetic sense as your guide, grind down the two bead surfaces until  you've achieved a disk that's at least ⅜ inch (9.5 mm) thick (photo 18). If you rush this step, you risk creating heat from the friction of the glass against the wheel, which can crack the bead, so stop frequently to wet the piece and make sure it's not getting too hot.

Finish the grinding process by using successively finer grits to remove the scratches in the surface of the glass. I usually use 325 grit, then 600, then 1200. Finally, polish the surfaces on a rag wheel charged with cerium oxide.

This portal is suspended on a head pin that is threaded through a hole made with a tungsten pick.

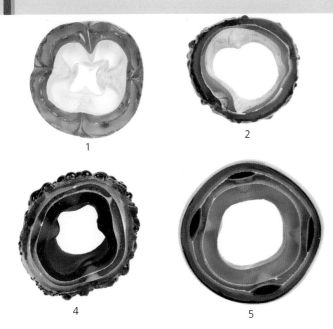

Project Testers

The Glass Portal ended up challenging the Project Testers in two distinct ways. First, the bead begins as a large, multilayer hollow bead, which was not within everyone's comfort zone. Second, that hollow is cut, sliced, and ground to reveal the artistry of the layers, requiring unfamiliar equipment and techniques. This is a labor-intensive and time-consuming project, but no one in the group found it overly difficult. Testers noted that the Puffy Mandrel seemed to make it easier to create larger hollows, both because they could be periodically re-inflated and because the warm air inside the bead may have made it less prone to shock.

A few members experienced what happens if you don't hang on to the bead during the grinding process. Emma's bead went flying across the room and shattered into "candy-like shards" **(PHOTO 3)**. A bead can also crack for no apparent reason. One of Jackie's hollow beads traveled safely from Israel to the United States, only to crack on my grinder **(PHOTO 26)**.

The Glass Portals of Kristen **(PHOTO 2)**, Jen **(PHOTO 1)**, Emma **(PHOTO 32)**, and Carolyn **(PHOTO 5)** stick to the color scheme and "tungsten-pick poke" of my example, and yet all achieved distinctive, lovely beads that don't look like copies, but rather like their own expression of the design.

Debby **(PHOTO 10)**, Jackie **(PHOTO 9)**, and Jen **(PHOTO 11)** all varied the color theme and explored opaque glass. Opaques can be a problem, because they don't always polish well, and in my original concept of this project, the portal was to be

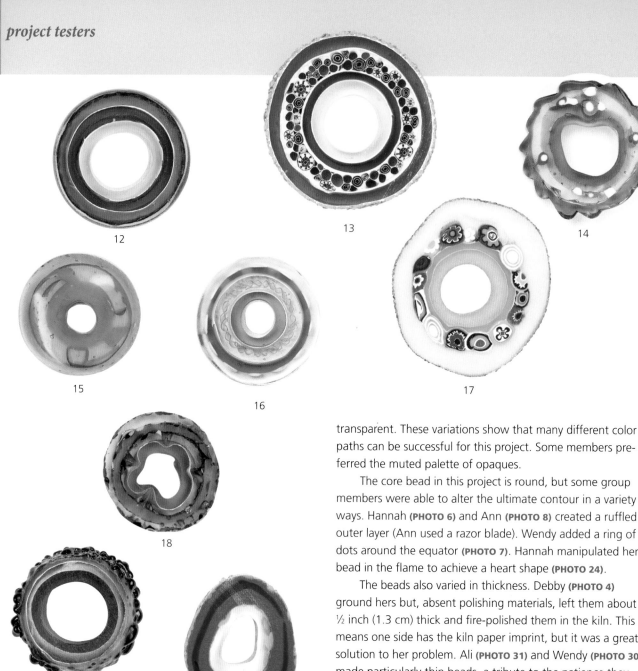

12

13

14

15

16

17

18

19

20

Ann Conlin, **21**; Sharon Driscoll, **12**, **14**, **15**; Carolyn Martin, **23**; Emma Mullins, **22**; Kristin Frantzen Orr, **27**; Jen Place, **18**, **20**; Hannah Rosner, **25**; Debby Weaver, **19**; Wendy Wilmott, **28**, **29**

transparent. These variations show that many different color paths can be successful for this project. Some members preferred the muted palette of opaques.

The core bead in this project is round, but some group members were able to alter the ultimate contour in a variety of ways. Hannah **(PHOTO 6)** and Ann **(PHOTO 8)** created a ruffled outer layer (Ann used a razor blade). Wendy added a ring of dots around the equator **(PHOTO 7)**. Hannah manipulated her bead in the flame to achieve a heart shape **(PHOTO 24)**.

The beads also varied in thickness. Debby **(PHOTO 4)** ground hers but, absent polishing materials, left them about ½ inch (1.3 cm) thick and fire-polished them in the kiln. This means one side has the kiln paper imprint, but it was a great solution to her problem. Ali **(PHOTO 31)** and Wendy **(PHOTO 30)** made particularly thin beads, a tribute to the patience they brought to the project. When working this thin, you need to be ultra-careful to keep the bead cool so that it doesn't crack from the heat of friction.

Sharon **(PHOTOS 13 AND 16)** and Ali **(PHOTO 17)** achieved spectacular results by including murrini, cased canes, or twisties in their portals. Each of them explored this idea independently before sharing it with the group. At the same time, I too was exploring the inclusion of murrini canes, which can result in a look that Sharon describes as "capillaries." The inspiring and aesthetically pleasing results speak for themselves.

21

22

23

24

25

26

27

28

29

30

31

32

Emma also had to work around a lack of a flat lap grinder. She was able to do the initial grind on a borrowed bench grinder. To finish the grinding, she spent "*hours* grinding figure eights" on a "sheet of plate glass, 220-grit abrasive, with dishwashing liquid and water" before polishing on a disk covered in soft leather. Talk about patience! But what a successful bead (it's at bottom right.)

Heather Trimlett
Anaheim Discs, 2009
Each, 1¾ inches (4.4 cm) in diameter
Cased stringer, twists; flameworked, ground, polished
Photo by Robert Liu

D. Lynne Bowland
Bubble Love, 2009
1⅛ x 1⅛ x 1⅛ inches (2.8 x 2.8 x 2.75 cm)
Soft glass, enamels, cane, goldstone; flame-
worked, ground, cold polished
Photo by artist

Tom Holland
Family Cane on Silver Foil, 2009
1¼ x 1⅜ x ⅜ inches (3.3 x 3.6 x .8 cm)
Soft glass; flameworked, flat lap polished
Photo by Becky Dahlstedt

Laura L. Bowker
Groovin' Blue, 2010
1 x 1⅜ x 1⅜ inches (2.5 x 3.5 x 3.5 cm)
Soft glass; lampworked, coldworked, battuto
engraving technique
Photo by artist

Dawn M. Lombard
Southwest Sunset, 2009
2 x ⅜ x ½ inches (5.2 x 1 x 1.3 cm)
Borosilicate; ground, faceted
Photo by Patrick Manning

Pinar Hakim
Sienna, 2010
Beads each ¾ to 1 inch (1.9 cm to 2.5 cm) in diameter
Glass; silver; hollow blown, cold cut, sandblasted, etched
Photo by Eli Hakim

Frank Scott
Botanical Geode, 2009
1⅜ x 1 x ⅝ inches (3.5 x 2.8 x 1.5 cm)
Soft glass; flameworked, ground, cold polished
Photo by Bill Frantz

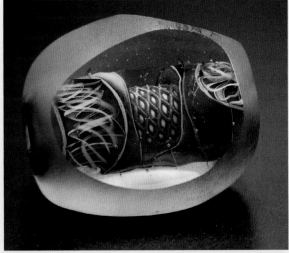

Petra Janssen
LiTE.NiTE, 2008
1¼ x 1⅛ inches (3.2 x 3 cm)
Glass, copper mesh; etched, faceted
Photo by artist

Petra Janssen
Time Is a Healer, 2009
1⅛ x 1 x ⅝ inches (3 x 2.5 x 1.5 cm)
Glass, silver findings; faceted
Photo by artist

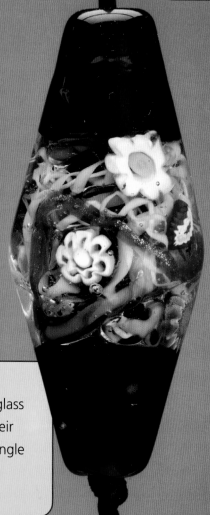

End-of-Day Bead

At the end of the work day, glass artisans sometimes use up their leftover tidbits of glass in a single project—just for fun.

What Will This Session Teach?

In this session, you'll learn to successfully encase murrini, stringers, and twisties in the center of a long bead, using a large volume of clear glass. You'll also acquire a few twistie recipes.

Glass & Materials
Glass rods ⒟
> Clear, 5–6 mm and 7–8 mm in diameter
> Pink filigrana
> Opaque turquoise
> Turquoise filigrana
> Opaque pea green
> Opaque orange
> Pastel medium lapis
> White
> Opaque yellow
> Light grass green
> Transparent dark cobalt
> Rubino oro (rose gold)

Gold aventurine, chunk the size of small grape (page 38) ⒝

Murrini, about 4 mm in diameter (page 25) ⒜

Tools
Basic hand tools (page 6)
Tubular, stainless steel chopsticks ⒞

Notes on Tools and Materials

Filigrana About 5 mm in diameter, a filigrana rod consists of a colored core encased in clear glass. This project uses commercially available filigrana. If you have none available, or if you can't find filigrana in the colors you desire, consider making your own by encasing a core color with a second, clear rod, and then pulling the resulting cane to the appropriate diameter. The colored core is about one-fourth the diameter of the entire rod, so the clear encasing is relatively thick.

Tubular, stainless steel chopsticks Excellent punties, these metal chopsticks provide a large purchase on the glass and last through many uses. Unlike soft glass punties, they don't soften in the flame. After use, they should be quenched in cold water while still hot, to shock off any remaining bits

> ### workshop*wisdom*
> Commercial murrini made with Italian glass (as opposed to the handmade murrini some artists sell on the Internet) uses a white glass that has a tendency to foam or burn when heated. For this bead, choose murrini with as little white as possible. Don't direct the flame onto the face of the murrini as you apply it; rather, wait until it's covered in clear glass.

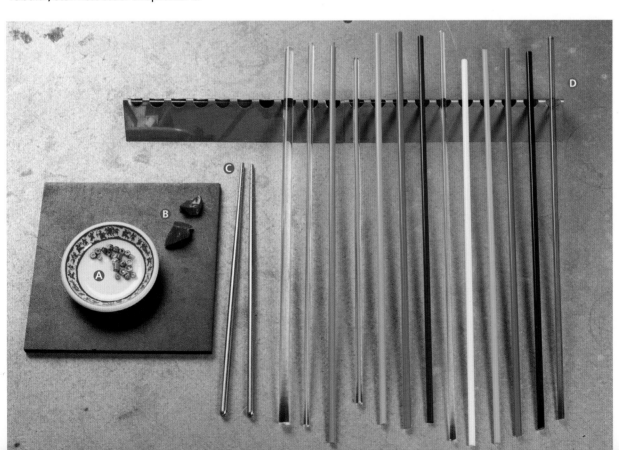

of glass. If you feel a gurgling sensation in the body of the chopstick when you introduce it to the flame, put it aside to cool and then throw it away. The gurgle indicates that water has gotten inside the tube, which will get steamy hot and *most* uncomfortable to hold. Of course, a borosilicate rod (which is ultimately completely removed) or a steel mandrel also works. Keep in mind that the diameter of the punty dictates the speed at which you twist the twistie—and thus the tightness of the twist.

An Overview

Some sources say that production furnace workers are permitted to use the molten glass left at the end of the day to show off their individual artistry. Here we cheat a little, creating our end-of-day components—little stringers and twisties—and using commercially available murrini. The components will be embedded in the center of a long bead and then encased with a deep lens of clear glass.

Over time, if you save up the bits left over from other bead projects, you'll have your own components, and your end-of-day pieces will become far more original.

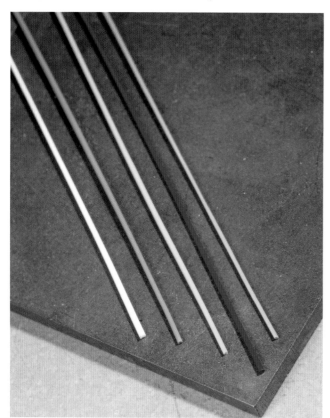

Fat stringers about 2 mm in diameter

Creating the Bead
MAKING THE TWISTIES

To make any of the twisties used in this bead, you'll follow the same four steps. (1) Pull a fat stringer. (2) Apply stripes of the fat stringer to a glass rod. (3) Use a chopstick to punty up the end of the rod. (4) Heat and then twist the striped rod into a tight and skinny twistie.

To pull a fat stringer, create a large gather of glass on the end of a rod, rocking it toward you and away from you as you heat the glass (photo 1). When the gather is a bit larger than a fat grape, raise the rod out of the flame, continuing to rock it to keep the gather centered on the rod. In about three to five seconds, when you see the gather stiffen slightly, grab the end of it with the serrated tweezers. Continuing to rock both hands in unison, slowly begin to pull the stringer from the gather (photos 2 and 3). To make sure the stringer is actually thick, pull slowly, speeding up slightly as the glass gets stiffer. To disconnect the stringer, use the flame to cut through the glass, keeping the cut ends close to the torch as they separate, so that they don't create long, wispy strands. These hairlike pieces of glass can make *nasty* splinters.

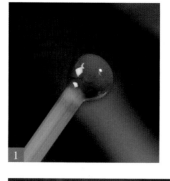

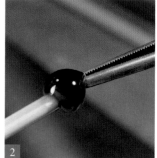

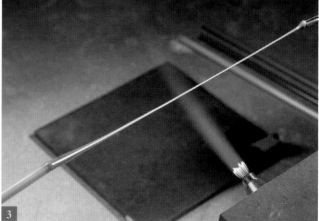

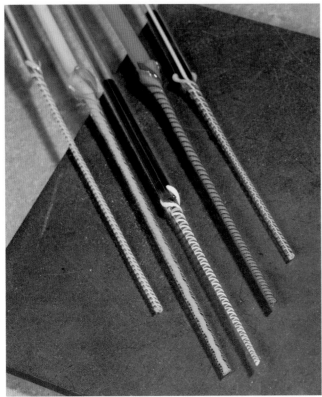

Each of the recipes on this page and the next will make a short, thin twistie—or enough leftover bits for several beads.

Pink Twistie

Using a rod of pink filigrana as the base glass, stripe on about a 2-inch (5.1 cm) length of the turquoise stringer at 12 o'clock and 6 o'clock. Punty a chopstick to the end of the rod, then heat the rod until softened, rise above the flame and pull while twisting (photos 4, 5, and 6).

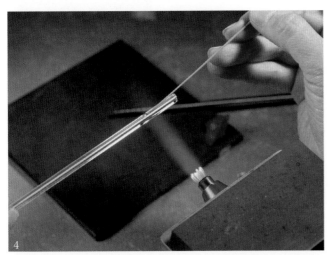

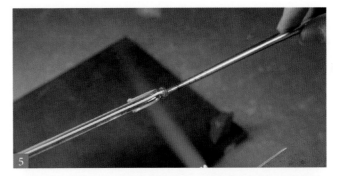

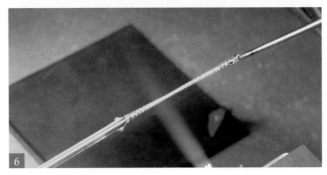

Turquoise Twistie

Using a rod of turquoise filigrana as the base glass, stripe on about a 2-inch (5.1 cm) length of the pea green stringer at 12 o'clock and 6 o'clock. Punty a chopstick to the end of the rod, then heat the rod until softened, rise above the flame and pull while twisting (photos 7 and 8).

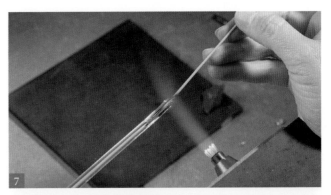

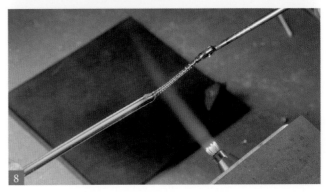

Orange Twistie

For the base glass, encase an orange rod in a layer of clear glass. Stripe on about a 2-inch (5.1 cm) length of pastel medium lapis stringer in three equally spaced stripes, at 12 o'clock, 4 o'clock, and 8 o'clock. Punty a chopstick to the end of the rod, then heat the rod until softened, rise above the flame and pull while twisting (photos 9, 10, 11, 12, and 13).

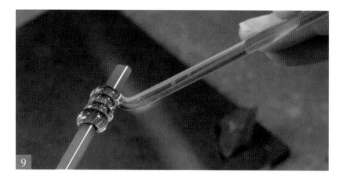

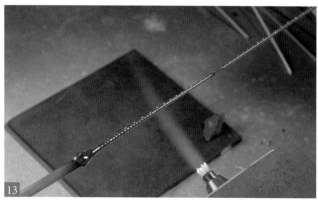

Clear Twistie

Stripe a plain rod of clear with two stripes of the white stringer, at 12 o'clock and 6 o'clock. Punty a chopstick to the end of the rod, then heat the rod until softened, rise above the flame and pull while twisting (photo 14).

Yellow Twistie

Encase a rod of yellow twice with clear, so that the clear encasing is about twice as thick as the yellow. Stripe on about a 2-inch (5.1 cm) length of light grass green stringer in three equally spaced stripes at 12 o'clock, 4 o'clock, and 8 o'clock. Punty a chopstick to the end of the rod, then heat the rod until softened, rise above the flame and pull while twisting (photos 15, 16, 17, and 18).

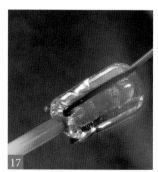

MAKING THE GOLD AVENTURINE STRINGER

You can purchase clear glass rods with aventurine crystals suspended inside, which can be melted and pulled into stringers, but we're going to create our own. For one thing, homemade stringers always seem more sparkly. For another, you can use any pale transparent color that works with your color scheme. Many years ago beadmaker Leah Fairbanks taught me how to pull aventurine stringer encased in rubino oro, and that remains my favorite combination. Many other pale transparents, such as a light amethyst or light green, also work very well.

If possible, preheat the chunk of aventurine in the kiln, so it's not too shocky (photo 19). If you don't have a kiln with an accessible door, rest the chunk on the edge of a torch-mounted marver, or on an electric griddle near the torch. If you decide you *must* use a room-temperature piece of aventurine, introduce it to the heat of the torch very, very slowly.

Begin by winding some clear glass onto the end of a chopstick (photo 20). (To get the glass to stick to the steel, bring the chopstick to a dull glow in the flame before wrapping it in glass.) Extend the glass slightly beyond the end of the chopstick, about the thickness of your thumb, and then extend it slightly farther by adding some rubino oro (photo 21). This layer of rubino oro will be the beginning of the encasing for your aventurine. I like to start with the clear and then add the more expensive rubino oro, so I use less.

Hold the chopstick punty in the back part of the flame with one hand, and with the other hand, pick up the chunk of aventurine with serrated tweezers. Waft the chunk through the coolest part of the flame, gradually warming it. Heat up the rubino oro glass at the end of the punty, and adhere the aventurine to the punty (photos 22, 23, and 24). Now that the aventurine is stuck to the glass, try not to heat it glowing hot; just keep it warm. Overheating the unencased aventurine will make it dull.

To begin the encasing, create a juicy gather on the end of the rubino oro rod and push it onto the aventurine. The gather should be very hot, so that it flows into any undercuts and crevices (photo 25). Continue heating glass and applying it to the aventurine until the chunk is completely covered. After

it's thoroughly covered in rubino oro, add some clear at the far end, where you'll attach a second punty. (You're doing this so you don't waste any more rubino oro.) Don't attach the punty just yet.

Introduce heat into the encased aventurine, to soften it. When it's soft, use large parallel mashers to begin to shape the encased chunk into a thick cylinder (photo 26). It doesn't have to be a precise shape, but by making the thickness uniform, you'll get even heat and an even pull.

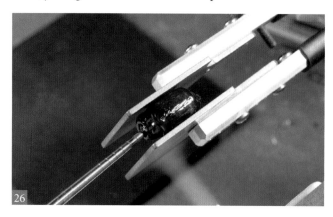

Now attach the other punty. Preheat both the tip of the second chopstick and the extra clear glass that you added to the end of the aventurine chunk. Then insert the tip of the chopstick into the clear glass, and wiggle it a little to make sure the two are firmly stuck together (photo 27).

Before pulling the stringer, it's important to get the aventurine core very hot (photo 28). This will require more heat than usually necessary to pull stringer. The chunk can remain stubbornly solid, and if you pull the stringer too soon, you'll end up with something that

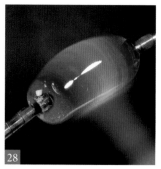

looks like a snake that swallowed a table tennis ball. To avoid this, direct the heat at the aventurine center, rather than at the clear glass attached to the punties, while constantly rolling the cylinder of glass toward you and away from you, to keep it centered and prevent it from drooping prematurely. Work your hands in tandem, so you don't introduce a twist into the gather of glass. Test the readiness of the glass by trying to bend the cylinder slightly. When it's very soupy, you're ready to pull. The final stringer should be about 2 mm in diameter (photos 29 and 30).

MAKING THE BASE BEAD

The base of this bead is a long skinny tube of transparent, dark cobalt glass with two conical ends, each less than one-third the length of the bead. The "open" center will hold the assemblage of glass tidbits.

To begin, wind on a tube of cobalt glass, as thin as possible and about 2 inches (5.1 cm) long (photo 31).

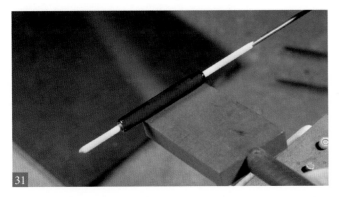

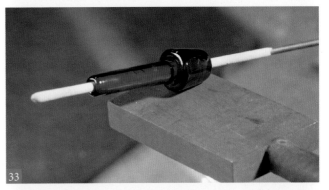

After the tube is finished, add the conical ends. They should be about twice the diameter of your tube at the end of the bead, and approximately three times the diameter of the tube at the widest part of the cone. This is like creating both ends of a bicone-shaped bead with nothing in the center (photos 32, 33, 34, and 35).

It's hard to keep a bead this long from cracking, because the part that's out of the flame cools quickly. You must constantly remember to keep heat in the ends. An advantage of this construction—making the conical ends before creating the center assemblage—is that the thicker ends can hold more heat, which gives you a little longer to play with the center of the bead before returning your attention to the ends.

EMBELLISHING THE BEAD

This is the part I enjoy most. Using the twisties and aventu-rine stringer, wind some decoration onto the center of the bead, in between the two cones (photos 36 and 37). Try to begin and end near the cones, where your starts and stops will be least noticeable (photo 38). (Alternatively, apply pre-cut bits of embellishment, which you can stick to the bead by preheating the spot to which they'll be applied.) Now is also a good time to put a single murrini in the center (photo 39).

Using the clear glass, add molten clear to cover the first embellishments and the murrini (photo 40). Try not to leave any air bubbles under this clear encasing, because they'll show in the finished bead. Adding the clear now, before adding more inclusions, will give the finished bead an ap-pearance of great depth (photo 41).

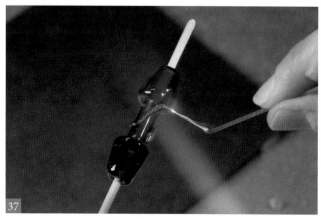

Add another layer of twisties, stringer, and murrini (photo 42) and then encase again (photo 43). This is sometimes called spot encasing: rather than enveloping the whole bead in glass, add the clear encasing to certain spots, as needed. Finally, add clear to give the bead its final shape.

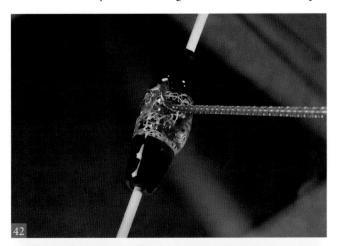

I've used a bicone with a softened edge as the center peak (photo 44), but a globe shape can be equally attractive. If you've encased carefully, adding glass where needed, there will be very little heating and shaping left to do to achieve the final shape of the bead (photo 45).

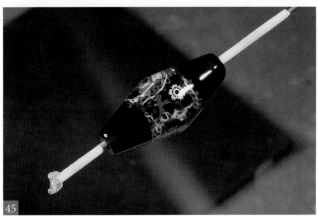

Give this bead one last overall reheating before popping it into the kiln. The goal is to bring the heat base of the bead to a uniform temperature across the varying thicknesses of the bead, which will ensure that the bead won't crack as it cools to the holding temperature of the kiln.

This bead represents the end of another day.

127

1

2

3

4

5

6

7

8

9

10

11

Project Testers

Every one of the Project Testers agreed this was the hardest project in the book. They all moaned and complained and struggled their way to a final bead, and few of them were happy with their results.

Many elements add to the bead's difficulty. It's large, it includes murrini, and it requires difficult encasing and shaping. Interestingly, however, the members of the group embraced not only my project bead, a bicone shape, but also the notion that this bead is made of bits and pieces of other projects. Many of their beads are shaped like the initial project bead, but they incorporate the leftovers that were uniquely available to each beadmaker.

Jen **(PHOTO 10)** and Carolyn **(PHOTO 11)** made blue bicones that evoke my project bead. A larger version of the bicone was tabulated by Ginny, and she made another into a square-sided barrel **(PHOTOS 1 AND 2)**. Ginny noted how important it is not to melt the little inclusions flat into the center of the bead, but rather to dab transparent glass around and onto the inclusions, to form the clear encasing.

Hayley **(PHOTO 8)** and Wendy **(PHOTO 9)**, who use a good deal of silver laden glass in their beads, used it to great advantage here. Unfortunately, one of Wendy's beads cracked after annealing, perhaps because of the abundance of barely compatible glasses she mixed into the interior of the bead. This was also a problem for Emma. Although it's not always possible to overcome incompatibility, I'd like to see each of them attempt the same bead with a deeper encasing and a longer and slower annealing cycle.

Sharon concluded that "more is more" and abandoned my somber color scheme for cheery beads that are heavily

12

13

14

15

decorated on the outside **(PHOTO 6)**. Ann also used a vibrant palette and "loved the randomness of all the different components" **(PHOTO 7)**. Jen was successful in adding external decorations to her beads, but was plagued by the difficulty of encasing murrini. Although she finished five of these beads, none of them truly met her standards. Jen feels "there is a lack of a focused design in the finished product" **(PHOTOS 3 AND 5)**.

Kristen dealt with the murrini challenge by placing most of them on the outside of the bead **(PHOTOS 4, 13, AND 16)**, for a starburst effect that the group loved. Kristen reports she used a 12 rib optic mold to make her murrini and 96 COE glass in raku and black.

Both Ali and Debby executed this project as a giant globe instead of a bicone. Ali finished hers with a two-tone bead cap and a metal core **(PHOTO 15)**. Debby made hers at the end of a mandrel and created a terrific bottle stopper **(PHOTO 12)**.

Emma hated working on this bead and said to heck with it. Instead, she made her usual end-of-day bead. She combined heaps of blue stringer with clear glass and mixed in some leftover frit, which she swirled with clear stringer. Then she added a frog, for which, she says, "I always have stringers handy" **(PHOTO 19)**.

16

17

18

19

20

21

Ann Conlin, **18**; Sharon Driscoll, **17**; Emma Mullins, **21**; Debby Weaver, **14**; Wendy Wilmott, **20**

Sara Sally LaGrand
Erin, 2010
22 x 3 x 1½ inches (55.9 x 7.6 x 3.8 cm)
Glass, wire, sterling silver; flame worked, wire wrapped
Photo by artist

Corina Tettinger
Pink Quark, 2010
2 x 1 inches (5.1 x 2.5 cm)
Soft glass; flameworked
Photo by artist

Corina Tettinger
Quark, 2010
1⅛ x 1⅛ inches (2.9 x 2.9 cm)
Soft glass; flameworked
Photo by artist

Michelle Waldren
Mardi Gras Bead, 2010
2⅝ x 1⅜ x ¹¹⁄₁₆ inches (6.7 x 3.5 x 1.7 cm)
Soft glass; twisties, cane work
Photo by Stewart O'Shields

Michelle Waldren
Mardi Gras Bead, 2010
2⅝ x ¹³⁄₁₆ inches (6.7 x 2.1 cm)
Soft glass; twisties, cane work
Photo by Stewart O'Shields

Mirroring with Silver

Mirroring can enhance glass beads in a number of ways. Inside a dark transparent bead, mirroring causes the color to appear super-saturated. A sandblasted surface on a mirrored bead can deceive the viewer into believing the surface is multilayered. Inside the bright colors of the Mirrored Rainbow Hollow (see Session 5, page 62), it produces a shimmering glow.

Ronnie Lambrou
Stardust, 2010
20½ inches (52.1 cm) long
Mirrored sandblasted beads by Jeri Warhaftig;
    crystals, Japanese seed beads
Photo by Panos Lambrou

Silver in a solution can be deposited onto a glass surface by gravity, or by coating the glass with something that attracts the silver and draws it out of the solution. When mirroring a curved container—such as the interior of a hollow bead—we need to take the latter approach. We coat the interior of the bead with a liquid—a tinning solution—that draws the silver out of solution and onto the bead. After the silver is adhered to the bead, an optional sealing coat of lacquer holds it in place and prevents it from tarnishing.

In addition to silver mirrors, chemicals are available that can produce either a gold-amber or a copper color. We're sticking with silver, but most of this information applies to the other colors, too.

SAFETY

It's important that you educate yourself about the materials we're using here, and that you take all possible safety precautions. Wear gloves, thoroughly cover all surfaces with a sheet of plastic covered by a thick layer of newspaper, use good ventilation, and wear safety lens glasses. Pay attention to the instructions from the manufacturer for disposing of the used solutions. Although this isn't considered a dangerous process and the gear may not be strictly necessary, it never hurts to be cautious when using chemicals. Read every MSDS (Material Safety Data Sheet) that the suppliers send with their products. Many of them can be viewed online before ordering.

WHAT YOU'LL NEED

Several companies sell silvering kits that include most of what you'll need: the chemicals for cleaning, silvering, and sealing; materials for disposing of those chemicals safely; and handy measuring containers. True, these kits are designed for mirroring beer bottles, but they're easily adapted to beadwork. Just scale down the volume of chemicals mixed at one time, and use a syringe to fill the beads with the necessary solutions.

Typically, the following materials make up a silver mirroring kit. (They can also be purchased separately.) See the photo on the next page.

Liquinox liquid glass cleaner Use this detergent to clean the glass and prepare it for tinning.

Tinning solution Sold in concentrated form, this chemical must be diluted with distilled water. In concentrated form, it has a shelf life of up to a year, but when diluted, it lasts only a few hours.

Silver solution, silver activator, and silver reducer After being mixed together, these chemicals are ready to use. (They're also available in bulk in concentrated form, which is less expensive, but because their shelf life is one year, always consider whether you'll use them before they expire.)

Silver remover You'll need to clean up any stray silver that lands on the outside of a bead.

Waste treatment kit This inorganic clay and polymer mixture lets you dispose of the solutions properly.

Lacquer This sealant is used to protect the mirrored surface.

In addition to the kit-friendly items above, you'll also need the following:

1 gallon (3.78 l) of distilled water

Latex or nitril gloves You'll use a few pairs, so buy the cheapest ones you can find.

10-ml blunt plastic cannula syringes Available from medical supply companies (many of them on-line), these are used to inject the solutions into the bead holes.

10-ml plastic graduated cylinder You'll need one for measuring the tinning solution.

Plastic measuring cup

3 catalyst dispenser bottles in 1-pint (500 ml) size Widely available on-line, these plastic bottles are also called MEK dispensers, because they're used to dispense methyl ethyl ketone. They're great because they measure and store the chemicals all in one container.

Small paper bathroom cups

Small waste container One-quart (946 ml) plastic take-out containers work well, but any disposable plastic container is fine.

Paper towels

You'll notice that nothing in this supply list is made of metal or glass—which would promptly mirror itself. Stick with plastic, paper, or latex. It's handy if you can work near a sink, but *nowhere* near food!

CLEANING THE INTERIOR

The recipe used here will mirror about six beads. If you want to mirror more, the tinning solution can be mixed an hour or two in advance, but the silvering solution works best when it's really fresh, so mix small amounts as you need it.

Dilute the Liquinox cleaner by combining about 2 ml of the soap with 1 cup (237 ml) of hot water in a shallow bowl. Add about six hollow beads, making sure they fill with the soapy water (photo 1).

Pick up each bead with a gloved hand. Covering the holes with your thumb and index finger, shake the bead with the soapy solution inside for about a minute (photo 2). After all the beads have been shaken, rinse them thoroughly with warm tap water. It's important that every bit of soap be washed away.

When you're certain the beads are clean, rinse them with distilled water. To do this, pour some distilled water into a cup, and draw the water up into one of the plastic syringes (photo 3). Holding the bead with one hole covered, inject the water into the bead (photo 4), shake it, and drain out the

3 MEK dispensers Ⓐ
Jug of distilled water Ⓑ
Container for waste Ⓒ
Disposable syringes Ⓓ
Graduated cylinder Ⓔ
Measuring cup Ⓕ
Empty measuring cup Ⓖ
Paper cups Ⓗ
Bottle of concentrated
    tinning solution Ⓘ
Liquinox Ⓙ
Disposable gloves Ⓚ
Old newspaper Ⓛ

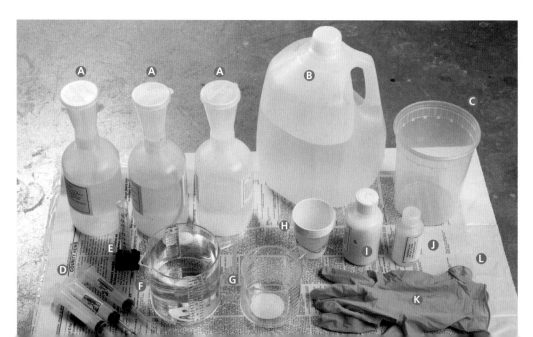

water. Repeat once or twice until you're sure the bead is thoroughly rinsed. Stand the beads on a paper towel until they're all rinsed (photo 5).

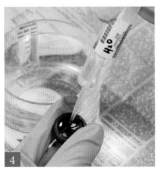

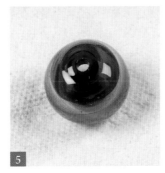

TINNING THE INTERIOR

Never prepare the dilute tinning solution too far in advance, because it lasts only a few hours once it's diluted.

Using the 10-ml cylinder, measure out 2 ml of the tinning solution into the plastic measuring cup. Rinse the cylinder with distilled water, pour that water into the measuring cup, and then add distilled water to the cup until you reach 2 ounces (60 ml).

To apply the tinning solution to the interior of the beads, draw up the liquid in the measuring cup in a plastic syringe (*not* the same syringe used to rinse the beads with distilled water after cleaning). Covering one bead hole, fill the bead approximately half full. Then cover both holes and shake the bead for at least 30 seconds (photo 6). Allow the tinning solution to drain out of the bead into the waste container.

Using the distilled water syringe, rinse each bead twice with distilled water, drain the beads into the waste container, and place each bead on a paper towel.

SILVERING THE INTERIOR

Squeeze up 2.5 ml of silver solution, 2.5 ml of silver activator, and 2.5 ml of silver reducer into the top of the dispenser bottles. Pour the measured solutions into a paper cup, and draw the combined solution into a new plastic syringe.

Inject the solution into each bead until it's about half full. Holding a gloved finger over each bead hole, shake it vigorously, in a number of different orientations, for 3 to 4 minutes. The interior of the bead will turn a muddy brown, and then the mirroring will appear.

Pour the used silver into the same waste container that holds the discarded tinning solution.

Using the distilled water syringe, rinse each bead twice with distilled water, allowing the water to drain into the waste container. Place the beads on a rack, hole side up, to dry.

If there are stray marks on the outside of the bead from silvering, they will appear as a brown haze. Clean this off, using the silver remover and a paper towel, then rinse both the inside and the outside of the bead with distilled water.

CLEANING UP

The silvering chemicals should come with an appropriate waste treatment kit—typically, an inorganic clay mixed with a polymer, which absorbs the solids from the chemical waste. The clay itself is dusty, like cat litter, so avoid stirring up the dust and inhaling it.

Add the clay to the wastewater. The solids will coagulate and drop to the bottom of the plastic container. The liquid can be poured through a paper filter and washed down a waste sink, and the leftover solids can be safely thrown away in the garbage.

LACQUERING THE BEAD

Once the bead has completely air-dried, you can lacquer the interior to seal and protect the mirror. This isn't essential, because the interior of the bead isn't exposed to many damaging influences, but it will increase the longevity of the mirror.

Draw the lacquer into a plastic syringe, and fill the bead about half full. Hold the bead in a gloved hand, with fingers covering the holes, and swirl the lacquer to coat the interior of the bead. Excess lacquer can be returned to the can for reuse.

Working with Resin

Although I'm no expert, I've experimented with various resins for use in glasswork. I've found several to be user-friendly and to yield wonderful results. In my search, I've relied heavily on the knowledge and advice of three artists in particular. Eleanore Macnish is a glass beadmaker and silversmith who has written about the comparative qualities of resin. Susan Lambert and Jennifer Place are both jewelers and beadmakers. Their input has been invaluable.

Resin for glass jewelry needs to meet several criteria. Besides being nontoxic and nonyellowing, it must provide a clear magnifying lens over the photo or artwork to be included. It shouldn't be water-soluble (to assure durability), and it shouldn't require oven curing, because a cold glass bezel would be shocky if placed in an oven.

workshopwisdom

When choosing a resin, consider whether you want a rounded dome finish to your piece. Some products are self-doming, but others aren't.

TYPES OF RESIN

Two resins meet these requirements: UV resins, and the two-part epoxy resins sold for craft applications. Both work well in glass pendants. Whatever type you use, wear latex gloves and eye protection, and work in a clean, dry, level space on a well-covered work surface.

Ultraviolet (UV) resins Sold in small dropper bottles, UV resins require light to cure (as in ultraviolet rays). Although they will cure when exposed to sunlight, that's not my preferred approach, because I work at all hours of the day and night, in a part of the world where winters are bleak. I use a curing light, which is sold for curing manicure products, but is also available from the same sources that sell the UV resin. These lights are a perfect size for beads or pendants.

Because they're pricey, UV resins aren't ideal for large projects, but I work small, and I prefer them. With UVs, I can pour only as much as I need from the dropper bottle, rather than mixing a two-part batch of resin and wasting some of it. I stick with the self-doming types, because I like that finished look. Other advantages of UV resin are the total absence of shrinkage and the ease with which mica flakes, glitter, and such can be stirred into the liquid.

Two-part resins Nontoxic epoxy resins represent a big leap forward in recent years. These new resins largely avoid some of the most difficult aspects of old-style resins: the tendency to bubble furiously and to be very messy to work with. There are still some bubbling and handling issues, but overall this newer generation is user-friendly after a few practice sessions.

Packing tape Ⓐ
UV light source Ⓑ
Bottles of UV resin Ⓒ
Embroidery scissors Ⓓ
Paper punch Ⓔ
Photo Ⓕ
Cleaned pendant Ⓖ

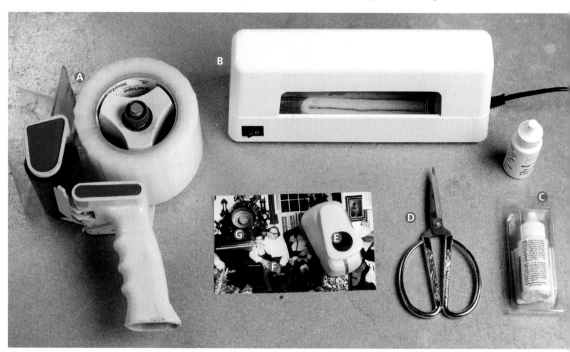

The two parts—a resin and a hardener—must be kept separate until you're ready to use them. Then they're mixed in a disposable container (such as a bathroom cup) and stirred with a disposable craft stick. Most of these resins are available in starter kits that include all these items.

It's crucial to measure carefully and mix thoroughly. The resin can be used for multiple pours for up to 45 minutes, when it will start to cure and become unusable. As the curing begins, the resin becomes thicker and viscous and will feel warm through the container. Depending on the brand, complete curing takes 24 to 48 hours.

SEALING THE INCLUSIONS

Paper inclusions should be thoroughly sealed before they're covered in resin. Otherwise, the paper will absorb the resin and discolor. I typically seal the image with either a white, water-soluble glue or clear packing tape.

To use white glue, thin it slightly with water, or use a product sold for that purpose in decoupage projects. Apply six to ten coats to both sides of the image and to the cut edges, allowing a few minutes for drying after each coat. *Hint:* If you work on waxed paper or a flattened plastic bag, the glue won't stick to the paper or plastic (photo 1). The glue will dry clear and seal the image.

To seal with tape, capture the image between two pieces of clear packing tape. With your finger, burnish the tape onto the image, especially around the edges, to make sure it's thoroughly adhered (photo 2). Then carefully cut out the image, leaving a very slight rim of tape around the edges (photo 3).

workshop*wisdom*

Some two-part resins are compatible with glossy, ink-jet prints, essentially high-quality photo paper. Even unsealed, this paper doesn't wick up the resin and discolor the image the way most paper does. If you aren't certain and the manufacturer's website is unclear, make a test piece before pouring resin onto your unsealed image.

White decoupage glue with foam brush **H**

Two-part resin **I**

Plastic mixing cups **J**

Wooden stir stick **K**

Squeeze bottle tops for resin **L**

ADDING THE INCLUSIONS

If you're using a paper image for your pendant, cut it into a circle that fits into the bezel, with a little room to spare (photo 4). (I'm using a paper punch here, but small scissors also work.) Seal the image and place it in the bottom of the bezel (photo 5).

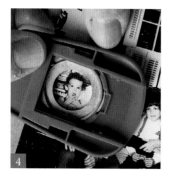

If you're using other kinds of inclusions as well—such as word magnets, charms, or dried flowers—now's the time to add those.

Be certain that your components are in place before beginning the resin process; if you use the two-part resin, you have a limited time to work before curing begins. If your components tend to float, glue them in place with a dot of white glue.

POSITIONING THE PENDANT

It's essential that the pendant remain level while the resin is poured and cured. The obstacle is that the tube bail on the back prevents the pendant from lying flat. Happily, there are many ways around this problem.

When I'm using UV resin—and want to fit the pendant under a fairly small curing light—I rest the pendant on the lid of a small box, after cutting out a window to accommodate the bail (photo 6). If the pendant still isn't level (which

means I didn't do a good job of making a flat back when I had it in the torch), I insert thin pieces of cardboard under the corners of the box. If I don't have a box that works, I rest the pendant on two blocks of Styrofoam or Lucite, so that the tube bail falls between them. Obviously, it's important to work this out before pouring the resin.

If you're using two-part resin (and thus don't have to worry about fitting everything under a curing light), you have other options. If I'm doing several pendants, I suspend them on a shoebox lid with multiple windows.

Keep in mind that with two-part resin, the pendants must remain in place for at least 24 hours, so cure them in a place that's dust free, where they can remain undisturbed. If you have concerns about dust, place a large plastic storage box over the pieces.

POURING THE RESIN

Both types of resin should be poured gently into the bezel cavity. If you're working with UV, fill the cavity about half full (photo 7), and then cure it according to the package instructions. After it has cured, pour more resin until it domes just slightly above the edge of the bezel. Then cure the piece a second time. With two-part resin, filling is done in a single step, and the piece is left to cure.

Bubbles are one of the main annoyances of resin. They're less prevalent in UV, but not unknown. Immediately after pouring, small bubbles may start rising to the surface. If this happens, use a straw to blow gently on the surface (photo 8). That's usually enough to get the bubble to pop. Another solution is to quickly wave the flame of a lighter over the resin, which brings the bubbles to the surface, where they pop. Since the two-part resin cures slowly, you should check for bubbles for the first few hours.

If the UV resin shows bubbles before it's fully cured (usually in the first few minutes after you put it under the UV light source), poke a steel pin into the bubble. If it pops and leaves a void, you can apply one last layer of resin, which will smooth the surface and de-emphasize the bubble.

Near Misses

Success is a journey, not a destination. The doing is often more important than the outcome.

—Arthur Ashe

The Near Misses embody my journey through this book. Normally, when I design a bead, I have a pretty good idea where I'm heading and what I hope the bead will ultimately look like. In designing the beads for this book, however, I conceived a set of *skills* that I wanted to teach. I then imagined project beads that would require and develop those skills. Over time, I created and refined the beads.

I enjoy the bead development process—refining a design, shaping it to be more aesthetically pleasing and closer to my envisioned goal. On rare occasions, a bead is terrific the first time I make it. (Okay, on *very* rare occasions.) More frequently, a bead passes through many design stages that inform the ultimate bead. Along the way, a heck of a lot of beads are made and set aside, rejected because of deficiencies in color, size, symmetry, functionality, or just lack of pizzazz. I saved them and share them here, warts and all, to encourage you to treasure the journey. (All of the structurally sound but not-right-for-the-book beads were donated to Beads of Courage, an organization dedicated to children with serious illness. Check out their website at www.beadsofcourage.org.)

RUFFLED PENDANT

The ruffling of the Ruffled Pendant started with a sort of winged heart. To foster the skill of heat control, I altered the design to move the ruffle farther away from the core heat of the mandrel. Early versions were embellished with palladium leaf, but because palladium blooms to full color only with a lot of heat, applying it was likely to sabotage the ruffle. So I substituted gold leaf, which requires less heat.

CHEERY LITTLE GUY

The Cheery Little Guy morphed through many different mouth styles, some of which were truly frightening. I learned to avoid making the eyes from murrini that were predominantly white (what a mess!) and fooled around with different color schemes. The sideways glance of the project bead ensures that he looks cheery, not shocked or startled.

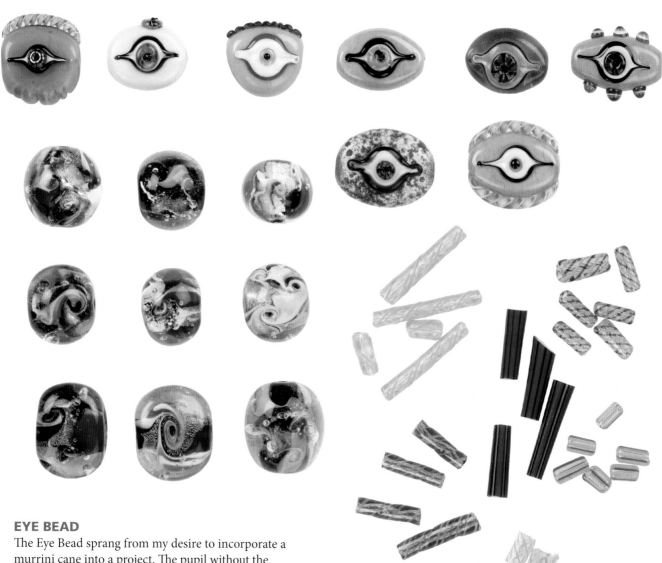

EYE BEAD

The Eye Bead sprang from my desire to incorporate a murrini cane into a project. The pupil without the murrini—which I used in some of my early attempts—resulted in a more traditional but less challenging eye. The versions embellished with complex twisties were interesting, but that technique was covered in my previous book, and I didn't want to repeat it. Ultimately, I upped the skill content of the bead by adding the aventurine-enamel background and the scalloped stripe as trim.

COSMIC BEAD

None of these beads are terrible, but each taught me something that ultimately resulted in a better bead. The top left Cosmic Bead is cracked; it taught me to deeply encase the glow frit. The remaining beads are experiments with size and shape, with different dichro, and with bluer and greener palettes. As a result of all this practice, I stuck with a black base, added more vortices, and covered the pale opaque dots with transparent glass, resulting in a darker, swirlier appearance.

CANE BEADS

My early Cane Beads were skinny, twisted, and made with transparent cores. To simplify the bead, I ultimately used a larger cabochon mandrel, a straight pull, and a white or opaque core. My near misses include attempts at different methods of finishing the holes. It took a little practice to fire-polish the holes without closing them entirely.

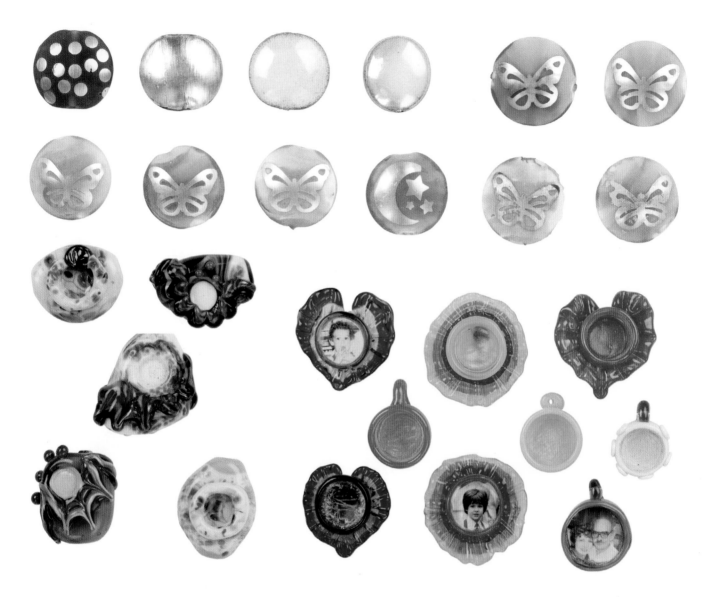

SILVER BUTTERFLY

The shape of the Silver Butterfly bead was never in doubt. Because the silver overlay paste needs a higher heat than the annealing temperature of the glass, I wanted a shape that was flat on the bottom, as insurance against the possibility that the bead would slump. You can see that I encountered many of the problems I discuss in Session 7: brush strokes that are too obvious, silver that came off with the resist, sandblasting damage where the silver was too thick. The moon-and-stars pattern was easier to sandblast, but I chose the butterfly in order to retain as much silver as possible.

GLASS MEMENTO

In the first generation of Glass Memento, I made round depressions in the bead with the flat end of a clean ring mandrel. I was unhappy with the result on many fronts. Because the mandrel was in the way, the depressions were too shallow and so didn't allow enough depth for collage elements. Unless the edges were built up with an even rim of stringer, the resin wouldn't dome. Plus, the colors looked as if I'd blended the Eye Bead and the Ruffled Pendant in a food processor.

After conferring with artist and friend Susan Lambert about my frustrations, I went back to the drawing board. With Susan's guidance I made some simple glass bezels and then branched out into the heart and sun motifs. The near-miss heart with the black and white photo has a loop on the back. The pendant didn't hang straight from the loop, so I altered the design to include a tube bail instead.

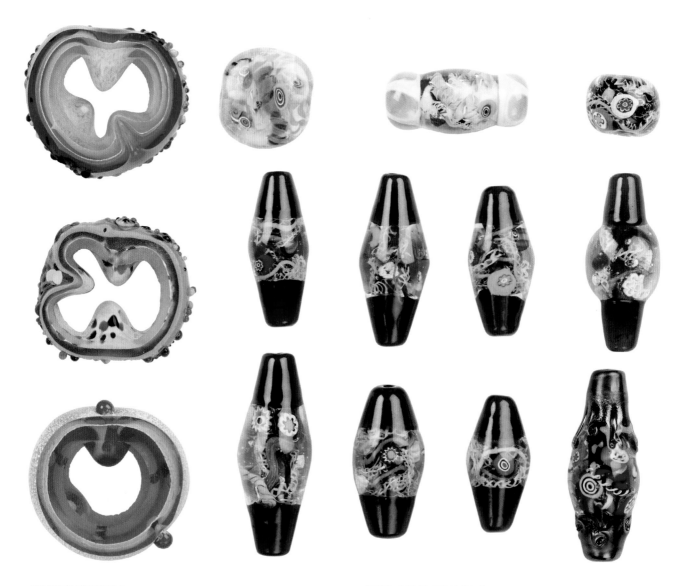

GLASS PORTAL

Because the Glass Portal incorporated two skills I had worked with before—making hollow beads and flat lap grinding—it wasn't hard for me to actualize my concept of this bead. The purple bead cracked when I let it get too hot on the grinder. The aqua bead is an experiment with dark frit. The one with the orange bulbs is an interesting idea for another time: thick orange stringer plunged into the funnels left behind by the tungsten pick. To me it looks like body-piercing jewelry.

END-OF-DAY BEAD

The End-of-Day Bead is the hardest one in the book—at least for me! The round bead at top right was the easiest version to make and embodied the primary skill taught by the project: encasing multiple components. But I ultimately felt that the longer bead was worth the effort, even though its heat-control issues made it technically more difficult. On close inspection, all of these near misses are decent beads, but I didn't like any of them enough to want to see them blown up to ten times their actual size on page 118.

The Project Testers

Ann Conlin, Massachusetts, U.S.A. Ann is known for her large focal beads and her love of all things silver: foil, mesh, wire, and glass. Her focals display her color sense and her use of patterning and surface manipulation. Having majored in glassblowing in college and worked for a time as a laboratory glass blower, she has a solid foundation in glass. Her beads have benefitted from studies with many leading glass instructors, including Jen Geldard, Andrea Guarino, Michael Barley, and Vittorio Costantini. Ann typically works in soft glass but has explored borosilicate, which she studied with Sally Prasch and Jake Vincent. She sells her beads online and at local bead shows. www.annconlinglass.com

Sylvie Dreyfus, Switzerland Influenced by such notable instructors as Kristina Logan, Michael Barley, and Jennifer Geldard, Sylvie has been torching since 2004. She prefers hands-on instruction, but she's also a devoted collector and reader of all things related to lampworking. After she has learned a new technique in class, she finds that the books enable her to break the technique into its component parts, so that she can practice each step. Although she doesn't profess to be married to any particular style, her beads are notable for the precision of their execution. If you befriend Sylvie, she will offer you chocolate. *Swiss* chocolate. www.sylvied.com

Sharon Driscoll, Michigan, U.S.A. Sharon started as a metal-smith in college but expanded into glass about 16 years ago. Although she has had many great instructors, she points to Sylvie Lansdowne, Loren Stump, and Jennifer Geldard as huge influences. Sharon is drawn to Day of the Dead imagery, which she has explored in many media. With her

excitement for every aspect of glasswork, she brought a sense of adventure to the Project Testers. She torches daily without fail and enjoys networking with other glass fanatics through the Internet and the Southeastern Michigan Beadworker's Guild. www.rightturnartwerks.etsy.com; delinquent.beader@gmail.com

Carolyn Martin, Queensland, Australia Located in the beautiful Mackay and Whitsundays area of Australia, Carolyn has explored

beadmaking since March 2005, primarily on her own, using books and online resources. She has enjoyed live classes with Peter Minson, Bernie Stoner, Corina Tettinger, and Loren Stump. Her beads are inspired by the colors of Australia and are executed in a free-flowing, organic style that she defines as "contemporary abstract." Rich with silvered ivory and silver laden glass, her beads are used by both Australian and international jewelry designers, and in jewelry made by Carolyn and her two sisters working in concert. www.katzeyekreations.com

Emma Mullins, New South Wales, Australia Emma chanced upon a newspaper ad for a two-day course in making glass beads—and the rest is history. She's now a self-confessed "bead-a-holic." Emma's signature motifs are sculptural frogs and florals. Although she works predominantly in soft glass, she admits to a weakness for the silvered glasses now available. She only occasionally sells her beads, so she donates to Beads of Courage to brighten the lives of sick children. A wood, metals, and agriculture teacher for secondary students, she hopes one day to incorporate her beading into her classroom. But her

ultimate fantasy is to spend one day with her lampworking idols all in the same studio: Corina Tettinger, Sarah Hornik, Anastasia, Lydia Muell, and Tom Moore, an Australian glassblower from Adelaide. em_marie1979@yahoo.com

Kristen Frantzen Orr, Nevada , U.S.A. After more than 17 years as a beadmaker, Kristen has a well-deserved reputation as a skilled artist and teacher. She has studied with numerous beadmakers, and cites Loren Stump and Leah Fairbanks as important influences. There's no question that her

elegant and precise striped cane florals are her signature style, and her work appears in collections throughout the world. Kristen welcomed being a Project Tester as an opportunity to "play instead of produce." She enjoys teaching college-level classes and weekend workshops, often expanding her own horizons in the process. www.kristenfrantzenorr.com

Jennifer (Jen) Place, New Jersey, U.S.A. A multifaceted artist and jeweler, Jen is as comfortable with metals and found object sculpture as she is with glass beads. She considers herself an "experimenter" who likes a new challenge. In the past 12 years, Jen has been captivated by glass beadmaking and has grown in her art by virtue of an intensive class with Kristina

Logan and frequent attendance at International Society of Glass Beadmaker gatherings. Jen combines her beads and metalwork in jewelry that embodies her signature style: large and utterly simple focal beads that show off very strong shapes in a single color, enhanced by oxidized silver. She enjoys figuring out ways to hold beads in silver settings and to combine glasswork with other media, such as resin. Jen and Jeri Warhaftig live near each other and frequently schedule "play dates" to explore new materials or practice new techniques. jencos@optonline.net

Hannah Rosner, New Mexico, U.S.A. For more than 15 years,

Hannah has been making lampworked beads with an emphasis on flowers and sculptural work. Her studio is nestled between the Taos Mountain and the Rio Grande gorge, and the inspiration derived from the breathtaking views infuses her work. She's known for her seed bead creations, which have won great acclaim, and has authored a number of tutorials that combine seed beading and lampwork. Hannah considers herself most influenced by teachers Loren Stump and Milissa Montini, but also draws on a rich background in the arts that includes an MFA in theatrical design and graduate work in glassblowing. www.goodrivergallery.com

Ginny Hampton Schmidt, Texas, U.S.A.
Ginny gave up life in the corporate world to pursue her passion as a full-time beadmaker. She teaches beadmaking, sells her beads and jewelry online and in bead shows, and handles

many custom bead orders. She enjoys precise decoration and the use of patterns, stringers, and dots. She's most influenced by the teachings of Larry Scott, an instructor who delves into the theory and technique behind a particular bead style. The only TV star among the Project Testers, Ginny was featured on an HGTV show about U.S. crafters. www.ginnovations.com

Hayley Tsang, California, U.S.A. Hayley's beadmaking trajectory took a big leap forward when, as a new beadmaker, she took a class with Kimberly Affleck. Since then she's been most influenced by Vittorio Costantini and Gianni Toso, who have piqued her interest in sculptural work. Hayley has spent a great deal of time exploring silver glass (soda lime glass laden with silver and other metals) and has written, taught, and authored tutorials on the sub-

ject. Although working with silver glass is her passion, her obsession is executing a perfect form, such as a bicone, a tube, an olive, a barrel, or a hollow. Hayley is a regional director of the ISGB and active in its many programs. www.envisionsf.com

Alexandra (Ali) VandeGrift, New Jersey, U.S.A. An early learner, Ali developed her love of beads while still in high school. Since then she's attained an associate's degree in scientific glassblowing, providing her with a wide range of knowledge and skill. Ali's beads are known for their organic appearance and wearability. She often uses a variety of presses and tools to tabulate her beads, and has only

just begun to refine her signature style. Her current passion is combining glass with silver. As a recipient of multiple scholarships to Penland School of Crafts in North Carolina, she's found she's

most inspired while surrounded by like-minded individuals. With this in mind, she intends to continue her education with the many talented teachers in the craft community. Aliveglass@mac.com

Jackie Waik-Atiya, Israel Relatively new to the art, Jackie combines her glass beads with her work as a silversmith to create mobiles, rings, and jewelry, some of which was featured in the book *1,000 Jewelry Inspirations.* She learned beadmaking from teachers such as

Sarah Hornik and Amnon Elbaz, and by actively participating in online forums. Jackie is especially fond of silver laden glasses, frits, and hollow beads. She shares her studio with a friend who makes glass sculptures. Jackie lives on a kibbutz in the Bet-Shean Valley, surrounded by date trees, migrating birds, three kids, three cats, one dog, and a parrot. eden13@bezeqint.net

Debby Weaver, Maryland, U.S.A. Debby took her first of many beadmaking classes in 1997 from Kate Fowle Meleney, and fell instantly in love with lampwork. She is known for her use of bright primary colors and for exploring a wide variety of styles. She admits that she will "put a bead on anything I can." Debby often works in collaboration with silversmith Beth Carey, a partnership that she finds really stretches her creativity. Her work has been in-

cluded in a number of beadmaking books and nationally juried shows. As a recently retired middle-school art teacher, she now devotes herself full time to making and teaching about lampwork beads. www.debbyweaver.com

Wendy Willmott, England Although Wendy has been beadmaking for only a few years, she dedicates a part of every day to time at the torch, and her work belies her brief experience. While juggling the demands of her young family, Wendy has pursued her art through continuous experimentation and time spent with beadmaking friends, lampworking books, and Internet forums. She is enamored

with what she describes as "clever glass," the silvered glass and reduction glass that provide the color that excites her. Her inspiration comes from her beautiful surroundings. Wendy lives overlooking a creek, which provides her with an array of vibrant insects and birds, and with the serenity of boats and still waters. Her finished pieces reveal the soothing pastoral color schemes that result from her beautiful environment. www.creekybeads-uk.com

Acknowledgments

I'm fortunate to be surrounded by loving and supportive friends, family, and co-workers who have tolerated my absence from other commitments and occasional (or not so occasional) grouchiness when I muttered some excuse about "the book". Many of them have pitched in with technical definitions, critical reviews, and re-reads of each chapter. In particular, the beadmakers who agreed to be my project testers were each a constant source of enthusiasm and feedback. I appreciate their patience, especially considering that some of them are well-established bead artists and teachers who agreed to be "students" for the purposes of this book. Our work together has validated my efforts in designing these projects and laboring over the tutorials.

In addition, there are certain people in my life who have nurtured me artistically and influenced me to pursue my work as a beadmaker and teacher. These are the people who are always there for me and catch me when I stumble. They have relieved me of my "to do" lists and reassured me that I can conquer seemingly insurmountable obstacles. Their generosity of spirit and love makes them my role models. I gratefully acknowledge the following people who helped clear the path for this book:

The members of the beadmaking community, especially those who labored to provide me with gallery images, new tools, and technical information. In particular, Ann Scherm Baldwin, Lori Riley, Craig Milliron, and Jennifer Place, who have been my sounding boards throughout.

My students and my teachers. The former have hopefully benefitted from my over-analytical and deliberate approach to my art, and the latter have optimistically tried to plug me into my inner creative flow while overlooking my ineptitudes.

Steve Mann, a consummate photographer and houseguest; Carol Taylor, a copy editor who is a writer's dream; Valerie Shrader, who encouraged me to pursue the concept of "project testers"; Kathy Holmes, who brought the pages to life; Nathalie Mornu, my editor, who got me to the finish line; Abby Haffelt, for her editorial assistance; and intern Maegan Zigarevich, who pitched in when there were technical difficulties.

My sisters, Sue and Linda, and their families. My beloved cousins, Caren and Ned Borowsky. Leah Ellie Holland, who weighed in on many of the project beads. Ronnie Lambrou, my dear friend whose astonishing jewelry makes my beads look so good, and her husband, Panos, who memorializes her jewelry (and thus my beads) in definitive photographs. My girlfriends, near and far.

My mother, Lorry Warhaftig, the mother everyone else wishes they had. She raised me with the maxim that every day must include one art project and has never scoffed at how much time and energy I devote to the frivolities of beadmaking.

My children, Jonah, Seth, Noah, and Ali. I am honored that they treat my endeavors seriously, that they are proud of me, and that their feet are on admirable paths in life. I take them just as seriously, and I'm very proud of them.

Most importantly, my husband, co-teacher and beadmaker, Neil Fabricant—Dr. Fab. After more than 35 years I remain in awe of his capacity to take on new challenges and master new skills. He taught me how to be generous and fearless and how to make small talk! I'm in love.

About the Author

Photo by Neil Fabricant

Jeri Warhaftig is a lifelong resident of West Orange, New Jersey. While practicing law full time, she has devoted her entire artistic life to handcrafts and, since 1995, has focused on creating glass beads. Jeri spends a great deal of time writing for bead publications and teaching lampworking in both the United States and abroad. She has also served on the Education Committee of the International Society of Glass Beadmakers. Jeri exhibits at major bead shows and sells her work through her website, www.jeribeads.com. Her beads typically reflect her frequent use of metal inclusions, chemical treatments, and cold working techniques. Jeri's most recent work seeks to push the boundaries of glass beads through combinations with other materials such as resins, metals, and found objects. Her first book was *Glass Bead Workshop* (Lark Books, 2008).

Sources

Check Jeri's website, www.jeribeads.com, to locate the tools and materials used in her books, as well as to find her teaching schedule.

Index of Contributing Artists

Unless otherwise credited, the beads shown in this book were created by the author.

Index